NOT AN EASY CHOICE

D0775353

NOT AN EASY CHOICE

RE-EXAMINING ABORTION

Kathleen McDonnell

Second
Story
Press

NATIONAL LIBRARY OF CANADA CATALOGUING IN PUBLICATION DATA

McDonnell, Kathleen, 1947-
Not an easy choice : re-examining abortion / Kathleen McDonnell. -- Rev. ed.

ISBN 1-896764-65-7

1. Abortion. 2. Abortion--Moral and ethical aspects.
3. Abortion--Psychological aspects. I. Title.

HQ767.M42 2003   363.46   C2002-904274-7

This edition © 2003 by Kathleen McDonnell

First published in 1984 by the Women's Press

Cover art by Lee Rapp
Text design by Liz Martin
Edited by Jane Springer
Indexed by Kate Forster
Assembly by Sharon Nelson and Irit Shimrat

Printed and bound in Canada

Second Story Press gratefully acknowledges the support of the Ontario Arts Council and the Canada Council for the Arts for our publishing program. We acknowledge the financial support of the Government of Canada through the Book Publishing Industry Development Program, and the Government of Ontario through the Ontario Media Development Corporation's Ontario Book Initiative.

  Canada Council   Conseil des Arts
for the Arts   du Canada

Published by
SECOND STORY PRESS
720 Bathurst Street, Suite 301
Toronto, ON
M5S 2R4

www.secondstorypress.on.ca

Visit the author's web site: www.kathleenmcdonnell.com

CREDITS

Grateful acknowledgment for excerpts from:

Abortion and Contraception by Henry Morgentaler © 1982. Reprinted by permission of the author and General Publishing Co. Limited, Toronto, Canada.

A Different Voice by Carol Gilligan, Harvard University Press. Copyright © 1982 by Carol Gilligan. Reprinted by permission.

Right-Wing Women by Andrea Dworkin, G.P. Putnam's Sons. Copyright © 1983 by Andrea Dworkin. Reprinted by permission of the author.

"Abortion: Some Ethical Issues" by Daniel Callahan in Thomas A. Shannon, Ed., *Bioethics*, rev. ed., The Paulist Press, 1981.

The Future of Motherhood by Jessie Bernard. Copyright © 1974 by Jessie Bernard. A Dial Press book. Reprinted by permission of Doubleday & Company, Inc.

"The War Against Choice: Inside the Anti-abortion Movement" by Deirdre English in *Mother Jones*, February/March 1981. Reprinted by permission.

Woman on the Edge of Time by Marge Piercy. Copyright © 1976 by Marge Piercy. Reprinted by permission of Alfred A. Knopf, Inc.

"Seizing the Means of Reproduction" by Pauline Bart in *Women, Health and Reproduction*, ed., Helen Roberts. Reprinted by permission of Routledge and Kegan Paul Ltd.

"The Case for Lay Abortion" by Connie Clement in *Healthsharing*, Winter 1983. Reprinted by permission of the author.

Letter from Vicki Van Wagner in *Healthsharing*, Spring 1984. Reprinted by permission of the author.

"The Right to Grieve: Two Women Talk About Their Abortions" in *Healthsharing*, Winter 1983. Reprinted by permission.

"Naming Our Experience" by Mary O'Brien in *Healthsharing*, Summer 1983. Reprinted by permission of the author.

"The Politics of Hysteria: Man, Media and the Test-tube Baby" by Mary O'Brien in *Canadian Women's Studies*, Summer 1979. Reprinted by permission of the author.

The Politics of Reproduction by Mary O'Brien, Routledge and Kegan Paul. Copyright © 1981 by Mary O'Brien. Reprinted by permission of the author.

"The Real Abortion Issue" by Susan Cole in *This Magazine*, June 1983. Reprinted by permission of the author.

"Cracking the Women's Movement Protection Game" by Lindsy Van Gelder in *Ms*, December 1978.

"The Ethics of Choice" by Rayna Rapp in *Ms*, April 1984.

For Mary Elizabeth Fitzgerald McDonnell
1906–1976

CONTENTS

INTRODUCTION
THE ISSUE THAT REFUSES TO GO AWAY
9

CHAPTER ONE
ABORTION: WHY A "RE-EXAMINATION"?
17

CHAPTER TWO
WOMEN'S EXPERIENCE OF ABORTION
27

CHAPTER THREE
MORALITY AND ABORTION
42

CHAPTER FOUR
MEN AND ABORTION
58

CHAPTER FIVE
"CHOICE": PURE AND SIMPLE?
68

CHAPTER SIX
THE ANTI-ABORTION MOVEMENT
81

CHAPTER SEVEN
CONTROLLING REPRODUCTION
95

CHAPTER EIGHT
RECLAIMING ABORTION
125

NOTES
141

BIBLIOGRAPHY
147

INDEX
151

PREFACE
to the 2003 edition

When *NOT AN EASY CHOICE: A Feminist Re-examines Abortion* was first published in 1984, it stirred up a great deal of discussion among feminist activists and the public at large. An exploration of what were, at the time, the unspoken issues in the abortion debate, it pulled together many of the current threads in the discussion and wove in some new ones as well. As such, the book was very much a document of that particular period and point in history. I continued to write and speak on these issues for several years after the book came out, but I came to realize that in writing *Not an Easy Choice*, I had pretty much said what I had to say about abortion and reproductive rights. As I watched my own two children grow up, the focus of my writing shifted toward them and the world they were growing up in. I began writing children's plays, young-adult novels and books about kids and the media, all of which I continue to do.

Yet this book has followed me with surprising persistence. For years after it came out, I continued to get letters from readers. They wrote about how much the book meant to them, and frequently expressed the sentiment that in exploring my own mixed feelings about abortion, I had given them the freedom to express theirs. And it wasn't only women I heard from. Not long ago I ran into an acquaintance, a man I hadn't seen in years, who praised the book and thanked me for making a space for men in the discussion of abortion.

Even when the book went out of print toward the end of the nineties, it continued to circulate. I received income through people photocopying parts of it, usually whole chapters for use in courses. In fact, since its publication there hasn't been a year that I haven't seen at least some earnings from *Not an Easy Choice* — an almost unheard-of situation for a book published by a small Canadian press. As I write this in early 2003, it seems that people still want to read this book and digest its arguments, and so it makes sense to put it out there once again.

I said in my Preface to the first edition that the personal catalyst for writing *Not an Easy Choice* was the experience of having a child. That child, my daughter Martha, has herself grown into a woman of child-bearing age, and her younger sister, Ivy, born in 1988, isn't too far behind. This new edition of *Not an Easy Choice* is particularly for my daughters and their generation, young women and men who never experienced the early struggle for reproductive rights in the sixties and seventies, but who might find it useful to know what we went through. Especially since they might have to fight the battle all over again.

— K.M.

PREFACE

THIS BOOK IS the product of a very personal "re-examination" of my own thinking on abortion over the past several years. At many points in this process, I felt a bit like a feminist heretic, attending pro-choice rallies and marches while secretly harbouring thoughts and feelings that seemed to clash with what I saw as the official "line" on abortion. Gradually I found myself coming back to a basic feminist truth: that our "politics" cannot afford to be divorced from our authentic feelings, no matter how vague or contradictory they may seem. Our real task is to search out and find ways to reconcile the two.

Unlike many of the women whose comments appear in this book, the chief catalyst for my own re-examination of abortion was not an abortion itself, but the experience of having a child. I have heard women say that giving birth to a wanted child only reinforces the strength of their commitment to women's right to choose abortion. The same was true for me, but the intensely involving experiences of pregnancy, labour, birth and parenting made the emotional context of such a choice infinitely more varied and complex. The birth of my daughter in the fall of 1981 gave the idea of the fetus in the womb a new concreteness: I marvelled that I now looked with such love on what "it" had become, and I could no longer easily separate the two.

Looking back, I can see that the painful confusion I sometimes felt was a creative confusion, a necessary stage in the process of coming to a deeper understanding of the issue of abortion. What was crucial in helping me sort through the confusion was the discovery, as I began to talk to other women, that I was not alone. On the contrary, I found that my developing views on abortion were part of a larger phenomenon that needed to be given a voice. The heartening response to an article of mine published in the Women's Press anthology *Still*

Ain't Satisfied in 1982, which raised some of the concerns and questions found in this book, also gave me courage to continue my explorations.

Thinking and talking about abortion no longer throws me into that painful confusion. I now feel a renewed clarity, and I am more committed than ever to a woman's right to control her own body. That does not mean, however, that for me the issue is closed. If anything, as this book argues in several places, many aspects of the abortion issue are becoming more, not less complex. But it is the complex, difficult issues that call on our best energies, that push us beyond our accustomed assumptions and values to a new synthesis. My own belief is that the ambivalent, paradoxical nature of abortion will always be with us, and that this is in many ways a good thing. What we need, if we are to avoid getting stuck at impasses as we explore some of these thorny questions, is new ways of thinking and talking about abortion. I hope that this book will play a part in stimulating that discussion.

—K.M.

ACKNOWLEDGEMENTS

I received much help and support along the way as I worked on this book, from many people who may not have been aware of it at the time. In particular, conversations and interviews with the following people at key points in my work helped clarify my thoughts and buoy my spirits: Rona Achilles, Mary Anderson, Fran Bloomfield, Betty Burcher, Connie Clement, Ann Rochon Ford, Shelley Glazer, Jennifer Penney, Judi Pustil, Tama Soble, Virginia Smith, Vicki Van Wagner, Francine Volker and Barb Young.

Thanks also to Shelley Gavigan for allowing me to read her Master of Laws thesis.

Special thanks to Connie Clement and Rona Achilles, who read earlier drafts of the manuscript and gave helpful criticism.

I am grateful to the members of the Women's Press trade manuscript group, who supported the book from its inception: Kate Forster, Connie Guberman, Liz Martin, Sharon Nelson, Lois Pike, Margie Wolfe and Carolyn Wood. Thanks also to Carolyn Wood for editing suggestions, and to Irit Shimrat for word processing and helpful comments. Kate Forster's copyediting and indexing were also important contributions.

Special thanks to Jane Springer, an excellent editor and good friend, for making the editing process such a positive one for me.

I am grateful to the Ontario Arts Council for financial assistance during the research and writing of this book.

For their personal support, my thanks go to Jim McNamara, who helped "midwife" the book in the early stages, and to Kay Brett.

Finally, to Alec Farquhar, for loving support, and to Martha Farquhar-McDonnell, for continually lightening the load — thank you.

2003 Edition

Thanks again to Connie Clement, nearly two decades on, for her valuable feedback on this new edition.

THE ISSUE THAT REFUSES TO GO AWAY

THEY WERE EVERYWHERE.

Over 200,000 young men and women wearing identical canvas backpacks, red and tan with a fashionably wide strap over one shoulder. In the summer of 2002, young Catholics from all over the world could be seen, in small clusters and large groups, on every street and at every intersection in downtown Toronto. Dubbed "pilgrims" by church officials, these young people had come to attend World Youth Day — actually a four-day event with a buildup that lasted several weeks — to which the local media gave blanket coverage for most of the month of July. Toronto residents frequently commented on how polite and well-behaved the World Youth Day participants were, with the unspoken sentiment being how different they were from the general view of young people as raucous, foul-mouthed troublemakers.

I was raised in the Roman Catholic Church. Many of my strongest childhood memories are religious ones — the nuns who taught me right through high school, the whispered darkness of the confessional, the haunting Gregorian chants and statues wrapped in purple during Holy Week. But as a teenager in the sixties, I rejected the Church along with a lot of the other values I'd grown up with. As soon as I was old enough to decide for myself, I stopped going to Sunday mass and joined the ranks of what the nuns used to solemnly characterize as "fallen-away Catholics."

For all that, I think it's true that you can take the girl out of the church, but you never completely take the church out of the girl. My Catholic heritage still stirs up powerful feelings in me, and I found myself in a state of vague agitation throughout World Youth Day. All this unabashed fervour, all this talk of the Pope as, in the words of one participant, "the nearest I'll ever get to Jesus Christ," made me nervous. Still, they dressed and acted like regular kids, not much different from my own daughters and their friends. They talked with great feeling about the need for peace and love and tolerance in the world, and one day I saw dozens of them dancing in the fountain at Toronto City Hall, looking for all the world like members of Woodstock Nation. Really, I chided myself, only a confirmed cynic could object to such a gathering.

That was before I saw the placard.

It had been thrown into a public garbage bin near the entrance to the Toronto Island ferry docks — a cardboard poster that spelled out a familiar anti-abortion slogan in large letters. I was a bit surprised to find it, since I'd been following the events leading up to World Youth Day very closely in the media and hadn't noticed any events with an anti-abortion focus. After some searching on the Internet, I discovered that there had indeed been a gathering on the Island a couple of days earlier, sponsored by a group called World Youth for Life. Billed as the "Pro-life kick-off to World Youth Day," it featured a Celtic rock band, Irish step dancers and a slew of anti-abortion speakers. Because it took place before the formal opening ceremonies, it wasn't considered an "official" part of World Youth Day and wasn't listed in the program. Which wasn't surprising, given the church hierarchy's desire to play down anything that might cause controversy and detract from the feel-good nature of the event.

Not that the abortion issue was completely absent from the main festivities. Archbishop George Pell caused a stir when he told one World Youth Day forum that he regarded abortion as a greater evil than the sexual abuse of children by priests. His remarks only served to magnify the general perception of the hierarchy's lack of contrition (to use a time-honored Catholic term) for the wave of sex scandals that have rocked the church in recent years. It didn't help Pell's credibility that, subsequent to World Youth Day, he himself became the subject of abuse allegations in his native Australia. And he certainly proved to be out of step with the public at large. When the *Toronto Star* ran a phone poll asking whether people agreed with the Archbishop's stance, a resounding 78 percent voted No.

The Catholic hierarchy is well aware that the church is losing the battle for public opinion on abortion, even among its own membership. Whatever their personal views on abortion, few Catholics agree with the church's position that it should be outlawed in all cases. Studies have shown that Catholic women are just as likely as women in the general population to have abortions, and Catholic countries — even ones such as Brazil where abortion is illegal — have abortion rates similar to those of non-Catholic countries. In the face of this growing worldwide acceptance of abortion as a fact of life, the church fathers have their work cut out for them. Events like World Youth Day are a crucial part of their efforts to re-assert control, to put forward the church's absolutist position on abortion and to mold the views of the upcoming generation.

Youth itself is no stranger to absolutism, and most adults have at one time or another experienced the lash of young people's scrutiny, their tendency to see things in black-and-white terms. It's an impulse that is part and parcel of youthful idealism — another way in which World Youth Day participants were like young people everywhere. My own belief is that many young people, particularly children and young teens, gravitate naturally to the anti-abortion position because it hits so close to home. They're disturbed by the idea that a woman can just do away with an unwanted pregnancy; it stirs up other unsettling thoughts in their minds ("Maybe my mother felt that way about me"). Given the complicated emotions around motherhood that are a part of growing up, I think these kinds of reactions are perfectly understandable and age-appropriate. And certainly many youths outgrow their absolutism, coming to appreciate the moral complexities of life, and of issues like abortion in particular.

Of course, Catholicism isn't the only enemy of choice. Christian fundamentalists and other right-wing conservatives have played their part, and there are indications that these groups are gearing up for a new round in their battle to dismantle the hard-won gains of reproductive rights advocates. In the United States, President George W. Bush has approved legislation making unborn children eligible for funding under the national Child Health Insurance Program, a move viewed by many as a major step toward having the fetus declared a person under the law. Pro-choice activists expect that as the current members of the U.S. Supreme Court retire Bush will appoint new justices with anti-abortion views, with the ultimate aim of overturning *Roe* v. *Wade*, the historic 1973 decision that granted American women the right to abortion.

Significant differences between the political climates of the U.S. and Canada affect the abortion issue. The so-called "family values" agenda that holds such sway in the U.S. is more marginal in Canada. It has become fashionable on both sides of the border to poke fun at the stereotype of the ultra-polite, middle-of-the-road Canadian, but in the political arena, at least, Canadians really don't care for extremes. The reign of the pro-choice (and avowedly centrist) Liberals at the federal level shows every sign of outliving the retirement of longtime prime minister Jean Chrétien. Even in the unlikely event that the Canadian Alliance, the only far-right party of any consequence at the federal level, came to power, they'd be reluctant to launch a wholesale assault on abortion rights. As right-wing provincial governments (including in my home province of Ontario) have learned, the way to hang on to power in this country is to distance themselves from "social" conservatism, sticking to hot-button economic issues like tax cuts and welfare reform instead. In fact, should the U.S. Right succeed in overturning *Roe* v. *Wade*, we might be facing a replay of the border scenario from the Vietnam war era — only this time, instead of serving as a haven for draft dodgers and war resisters, Canada would be a haven for women seeking reproductive choice.

Back when *Not an Easy Choice* was first published, I was apprehensive about how my colleagues in the pro-choice movement would react to the book's call to re-examine abortion. There were real fears that it would amount to "washing our dirty linen in public," that bringing these aspects of the debate out into the open would only give ammunition to our opponents. At one conference, Dr. Henry Morgentaler, the hero of the abortion rights movement in Canada, came up to me and said he'd heard from other activists that I had "gone over to the other side," but after reading the book, he was reassured that this wasn't the case. At the time, I felt it was important for feminists to try and counter the popular perception that we didn't think about these things, that we were cavalier about something that most people felt was a matter of grave importance. In the end, I think the book helped strengthen the pro-choice movement — by shifting the terms of the public discussion, by opening up new ways of talking about abortion.

It will be obvious to readers that many things have changed since the book was first published. The battleground has certainly shifted. Back in 1984 I wrote that I'd found some people in the anti-abortion camp honest and thoughtful in their views. I even speculated that feminists might explore some common ground with these people on other social issues — a suggestion that, given today's far more polarized climate, now strikes me as naive. Back then, pro-lifers regularly picketed abortion clinics, harassing and threatening clinic workers. Still, who could have guessed that some would go to the extremes of murdering abortion providers like Dr. Barnett Slepian, who was killed by a sniper in Buffalo, New York in 1998, or Canada's Dr. Garson Romalis, who has survived two separate attempts on his life, one in 1994 and the other in 2000?

Methods of abortion delivery have changed as well. In the mid-eighties, abortions were mostly performed in hospitals, whereas now they're provided in freestanding clinics. And while vacuum suction is still the method of choice, non-surgical or "medical" abortions have become available with the use of drugs like RU-486. When RU-486 was approved for use in the U.S. in 2000 under the name Mifeprex (at the time of this writing, RU-486 is not available in Canada), there were high hopes that it would bring about a revolution in the way abortion is provided. But so far this hasn't proven true. Since Mifeprex requires two or three doctor visits and often causes bleeding and cramping, women have found it more bothersome than the relatively quick, one-stop surgical abortion, with the result that the drug currently accounts for only a fraction of abortions performed in the U.S. There is also the option of the emergency contraceptive pill (ECP), commonly known as the morning-after pill, which is readily available in many countries.

The latest improvement in this area is a synthetic progestin, levonorgestrel, which is being marketed under the name Plan B. Many doctors give out open-ended "just in case" prescriptions for emergency contraception, and in a few jurisdictions pharmacists can dispense these drugs without a doctor's prescription. But Plan B shares the limitation of earlier forms of emergency contraception, which is that it must be taken within seventy-two hours after intercourse to be effective.

Even with all their drawbacks, non-surgical methods like RU-486 and ECPs could well prove to be vital options if the Right succeeds in overturning *Roe* v. *Wade* and outlawing abortion in the U.S. The very fact that these drugs work without the aid of sophisticated medical equipment, so that women can use them in the privacy of their homes, means that enforcing a ban on their use would be next to impossible. The fact that abortions were illegal prior to the 1970s certainly didn't prevent women from having them, and an underground market for abortion drugs would be even more difficult to suppress than the illegal backstreet clinics of earlier eras. The anti-choice movement may well succeed in making abortion more difficult to obtain for a time. But it won't be possible for them to truly turn back the clock on reproductive choice, for the simple reason that women won't allow it.

What, then, does choice look like in 2003? I stressed in the earlier edition of this book that choice was anything but "pure and simple," but now, in the age of reprotech, it is infinitely more complex. Indeed, in many ways, it's like we're living on a different planet. Back in 1981, amniocentesis was just becoming commonplace, and I was one of the last generation of women not to receive a routine ultrasound during my pregnancy. Now genetic screening and selective abortion for Down syndrome, as well as a host of other conditions, have become standard procedure. Yet the moral and social problems raised by this trend, especially regarding the rights and value of disabled people in our society, remain as knotty and unresolved as ever. Genetic screening may give us more "choice," but it has also made parents more reluctant to settle for offspring they regard as less than perfect.

We're faced with a similar dilemma in the case of abortion for purposes of sex selection, a practice that has been documented in a number of countries — most notably China, where it has been used for decades to abort girls under the country's one-child policy. Though there's no evidence it is yet occurring to any great extent elsewhere, clinics in developed countries are encountering more and more parents who want "one of each," and are willing to pay for techniques that increase their chances of having children of one sex or the other. In any case, advances in reproductive technology are bringing about a situation in which sex selection, and, to a lesser extent, genetic screening are achieved by procedures carried out prior to fertilization. This means that abortion will figure less and less into the equation, though the social and bioethical issues remain just as pressing.

Another area of contention unforeseen back in the eighties concerns the use of stem cells in the treatment of Parkinson's and other diseases. Research over the past few decades has demonstrated the remarkable regenerative power of these building-block cells, and the best source of stem cells is human embryos from fertility labs. Given the pro-life view that embryos have full personhood from conception, it's not surprising that anti-abortion groups have bitterly opposed the medical use of stem cells. In 2001 they successfully lobbied President Bush to block federal funding for stem cell research. This extreme position aside, there are some very real ethical issues in the stem cell debate. It's one thing to make use of "leftover" embryos, whose creation is an unavoidable by-product of in vitro fertilization. But what about the ethics of creating embryos specifically for the purpose of harvesting stem cells, which becomes a very real possibility as pressures for these treatments increase? On the other side, advocates for stem cell research make the ethical argument that the new treatments will prevent suffering and save lives. The issue has caused serious rifts on the Right, most notably involving former U.S. first lady Nancy Reagan. She has broken with fellow right-wing Republicans to lobby for stem cell research that could lead to a breakthrough in the treatment of Alzheimer's, the disease that has afflicted her husband, former president Ronald Reagan, for more than a decade. As so often happens in the swirl of issues surrounding abortion, when the political becomes personal, morality becomes much less hard-and-fast.

The eternal problem with abstract debates about abortion is that they stray too far from day-to-day reality. The fact is that throughout history, humans have struggled to control the number of children they have. When faced with unwanted pregnancy, women in past times turned to herbal abortifacients, primitive surgeries and even more drastic means such as exposure and infanticide. We no longer have to resort to such measures. Medical technology, problematic as it is in so many ways, has helped to free us from necessity and given us choice in childbearing. In 1984 I felt like I was going out on a limb in writing this book, but since then the views expressed in *Not an Easy Choice* have entered the mainstream. People are still ambivalent about abortion. They know that sometimes it's straightforward, sometimes it's messy and complicated, and often it's sad. They do believe that it's an issue with moral dimensions. But at the end of the day, they realize that the only reasonable way to deal with an unwanted pregnancy is to leave the choice up to the individual woman.

CHAPTER ONE

ABORTION: WHY A "RE-EXAMINATION"?

ABORTION IS ONE of the most volatile and contentious issues of contemporary life. For decades it has elicited an extreme, seemingly irreconcilable polarization unmatched by other social issues. On the one hand there is the loose alliance of feminists, leftists and liberals who argue for the individual woman's right to choose abortion. On the other, there is the self-styled pro-life movement, heavily influenced by the Roman Catholic Church and right-wing conservatism, which opposes abortion in all circumstances. These hard-and-fast political lines and the relative availability of abortion sometimes obscure the fact that abortion as a political issue is of relatively recent vintage. It has only been within the last twenty years that abortion has been legally available at all in Canada. Prior to that time the word was rarely even mentioned in public, and women were forced to seek out abortions in an atmosphere of shame and secrecy, risking their health, their fertility and even their lives to obtain a procedure they nevertheless regarded as essential to their own survival and well-being.

Throughout the sixties abortion reform groups mounted a campaign to pressure governments in Canada and the U.S. to liberalize or completely repeal their restrictive abortion laws. By the late sixties, within an atmosphere of change and social ferment on many fronts, these efforts appeared to have borne fruit in Canada.

In 1969 the new Liberal government of Prime Minister Pierre Trudeau adopted a number of amendments to the abortion section of the

Criminal Code. These amendments were shepherded through the House of Commons by then-Minister of Justice John Turner and legalized abortion in Canada for the first time since the early nineteenth century, when the first British statutes prohibiting abortion were passed. Far from making abortion an essentially private matter between a woman and her doctor, as most proponents of reform had long advocated, the 1969 amendments permitted abortion only under certain stringent conditions: continuation of the pregnancy had to be shown to endanger the woman's life or health, and the abortion had to be carried out in an accredited hospital and approved by a therapeutic abortion committee made up of not less than three staff doctors.

The much-hailed "reform" quickly revealed itself to be an unjust, unworkable measure that owed everything to the need for political compromise and little to concern for women's health or reproductive freedom. According to Professor Larry Collins, the 1969 amendment merely enshrined in law what had already become standard practice in many Canadian hospitals. For over a decade doctors had been carrying out abortions under fairly strict criteria, shielded by an informal hospital committee system that reviewed every application for abortion. Most hospitals where abortions were being performed prior to 1969 had adopted a daily or weekly quota, a limitation not mentioned anywhere in the law but which continues to this day. The federal government, according to Collins, opted for an abortion reform strategy that would not rock the doctors' boat, but would instead protect their "monopoly over the delivery of abortion services and ... the doctors and their hospitals from legal liability." In doing so, he argues, the new law accomplished nothing but the defusing of the controversy over abortion and the appearance that the government was taking action on the issue.

> The government's strategy was to attempt to ensure that no effective state action would offend any faction. Without legalizing abortion, the 1969 reform law enshrined the rhetoric of reform while basically just legalizing established medical practices.[1]

Abortion reform crusader Eleanor Wright Pelrine termed the new law "the reform that hardly was." Feminist groups, who had been active in the movement for reform, denounced the government's measure and stepped up their efforts to achieve their aim of free abortion on demand, organizing a cross-country Abortion Caravan in the spring of 1970 that culminated in a sit-in in the House of Commons. But the government's strategy was effective. It knocked the wind out of the sails of the reform movement at a critical time, saddling it with a half-measure that made abortion just accessible enough to neutralize pressure for outright repeal of the law.

It became grimly clear in the succeeding years that women in Canada did not win the right to abortion in 1969. The government's own Badgley Committee, set up in 1976 to examine the workings of the abortion law, found it to be unworkable, a bureaucratic obstacle course that endangered women's health by prolonging the approval process and increasing their anxiety about the outcome. By the late seventies, due to growing pressure from the anti-abortion movement and a political climate generally less favourable to women's rights, access to abortion had actually dropped all across the country. Some hospitals shut down their therapeutic abortion committees altogether. Many others reduced their daily or weekly quotas, or stopped performing second trimester abortions. Although abortion was supposedly legal across Canada, women were forced to travel long distances, often even to the United States, to terminate unwanted pregnancies. The situation approached a crisis point and appeared to be ripe for a mass political mobilization around the abortion issue. But this did not happen. Aside from intermittent skirmishes with Right-to-Life groups attempting to win control of hospital boards, the abortion rights movement remained relatively quiescent, to the extent that this writer could claim, in 1981, that "abortion is the forgotten issue of the women's movement in Canada."[2]

All that changed dramatically in 1983, however, when abortion once more assumed centre stage in the Canadian political arena. An irony for feminists lies in the fact that the abortion issue was rekindled in this country largely by the actions of two men: Dr. Henry Morgentaler and Joseph Borowski. In late 1982 Morgentaler, the hero of the abortion rights movement in Canada for his open defiance of restrictive abortion laws, announced his intention to open illegal clinics in

Winnipeg and Toronto. These clinics would operate along the lines of his well-known Montreal clinic, which had been providing abortions without harassment from the Quebec government since Morgentaler's acquittal by three separate juries on charges of performing illegal abortions in the mid-seventies. Around the same time as the first Morgentaler clinic opened in Winnipeg in May 1983, anti-abortion crusader Joe Borowski's constitutional challenge to the existing abortion law came to trial in Regina. Borowski's lawyers argued that the fetus was entitled to the full rights of a human person under the new Canadian Charter of Rights and Freedoms, and that the existing law permitting abortion even under limited conditions was a violation of those rights. Borowski's attempt to have the abortion law struck down was ultimately unsuccessful. Both Morgentaler clinics in Toronto and Winnipeg were shut down by police raids, and he and other clinic staff faced criminal charges in both cities. The effect of these actions has been to put abortion back on the political map in a way that has aroused more media interest and public sentiment than at any time since the early seventies.

Canadian feminists are now presented with an important opportunity to reach out to women and men on the abortion issue. How should we respond? In large measure, of course, we have already responded in the most forceful way we know, by organizing public forums and demonstrations and building public support for Dr. Morgentaler and the other clinic workers. These efforts have been effective in mobilizing committed feminists and advocates of abortion reform. Innumerable polls tell us that the majority of the Canadian public supports a woman's right to abortion, at least in some circumstances. But for the most part this much-vaunted majority does not choose to "vote with its feet" and prefers the anonymity of opinion polls. Furthermore, our majority support has still not resulted in the achievement of our goal: the repeal of restrictive abortion laws and the acknowledgement of the individual woman's right to choose abortion.

Is there something missing in the public discussion of abortion? Why has our feminist perspective not gained hold more strongly? On many other issues, among them rape, pornography and equal pay, feminists have had a tremendous impact upon popular thinking in recent years. The feminist perspective on these issues has actually entered the mainstream, where it meets with considerable sympathy, while the feminist commitment to the absolute right of women to choose abortion is still seen as "too radical" by most people. And it is indeed radical, as is the notion that women should control our own bodies. There is no way to soften the impact of that radical demand without diluting our stance on what is a bedrock issue of modern feminism. But can we perhaps search out new ways of talking about the abortion issue, add new dimensions to it – not to obfuscate or water down our perspective but to make it more accessible to many women and men we have not yet reached?

The fact is that feminist discourse on abortion has changed little since the late sixties and early seventies, when the contemporary women's movement first formulated a position on abortion and women's rights. This position has its roots in Simone de Beauvoir's pioneering work *The Second Sex,* in which she developed the theory that freedom from "the slavery of reproduction" was the pivotal factor in the liberation of women, a theme socialist feminists such as Stella Browne in Britain and Emma Goldman in America first posited earlier in the twentieth century. De Beauvoir documented in great detail the political, social and psychological constraints that women's long history of enforced childbearing had imposed on them, and argued that only with the ability to "master the reproductive function" would women achieve true equality with men and full participation in society. The other key aspect of the issue highlighted by de Beauvoir was women's sexuality. Women would not be able to express their sexual natures as freely as men as long as they had to bear the consequences of unwanted pregnancy. De Beauvoir advocated women's free choice on abortion, and the abolition of all restrictive laws, a truly radical demand in the late forties, when *The Second Sex* was first published.

These themes were picked up by the "second wave" of feminists in the late sixties and early seventies. The ability to control reproduction was seen as an absolute precondition to the political, economic and sexual liberation of women. The authors of the abortion manifesto in the Canadian anthology *Women Unite,* for example, stated that

> The ability of a woman to control her own reproductive processes is a
> necessary precondition if women are to throw off the bonds that have

for so many centuries stifled their full potential as human beings.[3]

Similarly, abortion reform activist Lucinda Cisler says in the 1970 American anthology, *Sisterhood is Powerful:*

> Without the full capacity to limit her own reproduction, a woman's "freedoms" are tantalizing mockeries that cannot be exercised.[4]

Although these early feminist texts laid a solid groundwork for a feminist perspective on abortion, little was done to develop it in the succeeding years. Much was written on abortion, both in Canada and in the U.S., but most of it was not particularly analytical, emphasizing instead practical and strategic considerations — what is an abortion, how to get an abortion, inequities in abortion legislation, and political action on the issue. This emphasis merely reflected the preference for action over reflection where abortion was concerned. Because so much energy has gone into fighting the Right-to-Life and maintaining what abortion rights we now have, feminists have had little time to think analytically about abortion. We have been too busy fighting in the streets and working in clinics and referral centres. What theoretical development did take place around abortion was confined to the introduction of the notion of "choice" in the mid-seventies and, later, the more comprehensive idea of reproductive rights, both of which will be examined more fully in Chapter Five.

Feminist theory in other areas has greatly expanded, developed and matured in the intervening years. Feminists have generated a deeply radical and enormously influential critique of violence in our society, for example, and have shown how it serves to perpetuate the exploitation and oppression of women in the form of rape, wife battering and pornography. The feminist view of the family and women's role in it has evolved from the anti-nuclear family sentiments of the early women's liberationists, to a more complex, multileveled vision, helped along by such groundbreaking works as Adrienne Rich's *Of Woman Born.* Feminists have developed an extensive critique of patriarchal thought and institutions, and have related it to the nuclear arms threat and the destruction of the environment. Religious feminists have revolutionized the role of women in established churches and the ways in which we think and talk about spirituality. In the general area of reproduction and women's health we have shown how sexism and patriarchal attitudes influence the kind of health care we receive and the kinds of contraception that are made available to us. Yet with abortion itself, we are still marching with many of the same slogans, and with much the same general position, as we did in the early seventies.

Is a re-evaluation of the feminist position on abortion really needed? Many feminists, including many active in the abortion rights struggle, would say no, because the issue is still essentially the same: the need for women to control our own bodies and our reproductive capacity, so that we can achieve full liberation as human beings. And of course they are right. On some level the struggle is and will continue to be exactly the same, until we have achieved real reproductive freedom. Others may argue that this is not the time to introduce new, potentially divisive elements into the feminist discussion of abortion, because we must pull together to combat the rise of the Right and a growing anti-feminist backlash. They are right, too. We do take a risk if we open up the agenda on abortion. Much like the current debate on pornography and the role of censorship, re-examining abortion holds the fearful possibility of splitting the women's movement and giving ammunition to our enemies.

But the most persuasive argument in favour of opening up the abortion agenda is simply that it is already happening. Larger developments in society are right now having a direct effect on the abortion issue and are demanding to be taken into the feminist account. If we ignore them we run an even greater risk: of becoming rigid, stagnant and ultimately irrelevant. What are some of these larger developments?

First, women's experience of abortion is not being addressed and integrated into the way we talk politically about the issue. Many feminists have long acknowledged privately that having an abortion is not the straightforward exercise it sometimes appears to be in our leaflets and slogans. Many women feel alienated from the women's movement precisely because they don't see these feelings discussed or validated. The Right-to-Life movement is talking about them, however, and is active in offering support services for women experiencing post-abortion grief or doubt. But feminists are the ones who should be talking to these women. We are the ones who can offer them real support and validation around their abortion experience.

Second, we are not reaching the great middle ground of people who have moral qualms about abortion. These are not the confirmed anti-abortionists, but people who simply feel that abortion does have a moral dimension that they don't see being addressed in the feminist stance. They may support a woman's right to choose abortion, but still hold back from full support of the feminist position for reasons they often cannot articulate. What many of these people need is simply the reassurance that feminists are as aware and concerned about the moral dimension of abortion as they are, that we don't regard it as a simple surgical procedure.

Third, developments in medical technology are radically changing the nature of the abortion debate. Our expanding knowledge of fetal physiology and psychology makes it more and more difficult to simply dismiss the fetus in the abortion discussion. The fetus is literally becoming a "patient" while still in the womb, the recipient of surgery and other therapeutic techniques at gestational ages well before the cutoff point for abortion. Advances in genetics and prenatal diagnosis are making abortion on eugenic grounds, as opposed to the social, economic and psychological grounds stressed by feminists, more and more common. How does this kind of selective abortion of "defective" fetuses fit in with our right to choose? New developments in abortion technology itself are impinging on the abortion debate, making it increasingly difficult to define precisely what an abortion is. Induced abortions are now usually performed some time after the sixth week of pregnancy, since it is difficult to accurately diagnose pregnancy prior to that time. A whole new range of "interceptors" – drugs or devices that intervene in the reproductive process *after* conception – is under development. Interceptors cannot readily be classified as either contraceptives or abortifacients: they do not prevent conception, but they terminate a pregnancy long before it can be verified, often prior to implantation of the embryo on the uterine wall. Many fertility experts consider implantation rather than conception to be the starting point of pregnancy, since they estimate that in the natural course of events nearly half of all fertilized eggs fail to implant and are expelled from the uterus. Interceptors are already in common use. The morning-after pill is one; so is the IUD, which is thought to produce a uterine environment hostile to the implantation of a fertilized egg. In light of all this, what, then, is an abortion? And how will we integrate these ever-expanding developments into our understanding of it?

Fourth, men are beginning to take on a greater role in every aspect of reproduction and parenting. A few men, backed up by the Right-to-Life movement, are beginning to talk about men's rights in abortion, and argue for male veto power. How are we going to respond to this threat to our reproductive autonomy, while at the same time encouraging more male participation and responsibility in birth control, sterilization, the birth experience and child care?

Fifth, some feminists are beginning to perceive a dissonance between our stance on abortion and our stance in other areas. Feminism has tended to ally itself with non-violence, with justice for the oppressed, with nurturance and respect for life and for the ecosystem. Yet abortion is in some sense an act of violence, and indisputably results in the termination of life. Is there a contradiction here? Possibly. It depends as much on how we define our feminism as it does on how we view abortion. For how much are these "nurturant" qualities a fundamental part of feminism? Some see them as an actual threat to feminism and to women's autonomy – the old idealized Mother Earth figure served up in a new but still oppressive guise. Others argue that the real task of feminism is to reclaim and validate these nurturant aspects rather than embrace patriarchal, male-defined values. The more we delve into these questions the more contradictions we find, but that need not frighten us. Life is full of contradictions, and facing them squarely and honestly can lead us to a new and deeper synthesis of our values and beliefs.

We need to do more than simply re-examine abortion. There is a need for the development of a much more comprehensive feminist perspective on every aspect of reproduction, including abortion. New reproductive technologies are now in place that call into question the whole nature of the reproductive process, and our key role in it as women. Some critical questions will have to be answered over the coming decades: to what extent will we choose to intervene in and exert control over the process of reproduction? For what purposes should we be doing so? And, most importantly, who will make the decisions? Who will be in control? The intensity of the coming battles over these questions may well make the fight over abortion pale in comparison. And an irony lies in the fact that Right-to-Life is one of the few social movements to explore and talk about the reproductive engineering trend with the seriousness that it warrants. Feminists must become intimately involved in this discussion *now*, before these technologies begin to see even wider application.

A re-examination of abortion is incumbent upon us. But, in a more positive light, it presents us with an exciting challenge, an opportunity to reach out to more women and men, and to deepen our understanding of both feminism and the reproductive process. Of course, we are simply talking about a choice to bring into our public discussions some of the questions we have discussed privately for so long. We are also talking about a shift in emphasis, a re-focussing of our attention on aspects of the abortion issue we had not given enough consideration to before. There is nothing in this book for which the seeds have not already been planted in the feminist view of abortion, and in that sense it is not really a departure. The truth is that there has been a need among women for this kind of re-examination, but it has been largely fear that has kept us from carrying it out — fear of where it will lead us, fear of creating divisions among ourselves, fear of our opponents using it against us. It may be a difficult and painful exercise at times, but we have to trust ourselves and our ability to come through it. We have to trust that our re-examination of abortion is really a coming full circle, and that we will arrive back at our starting point — abortion is a woman's right — but with a changed, deeper understanding.

CHAPTER TWO

WOMEN'S EXPERIENCE OF ABORTION

ABORTION IS AN issue that refuses to go away, and that continues to generate strong feelings on all sides. In Canada, the abortion issue has had its ebbs and flows over the years, surfacing in one place, dying down in another. Each time, it reappears with the same intensity, the same high emotional pitch. Unlike many other issues that meet initial resistance and become slowly more acceptable with the passage of time, abortion never seems to "cool down." Many pro-choicers are mystified by this. The idea of abortion rights seems so straightforward. It is the Right-to-Lifers, the opponents of choice, who are making all the fuss, as we see it, and if they would just go away abortion could finally be dealt with in a sane, rational manner.

Even a cursory look at the history of human societies shows us that this is an unrealistic expectation. Questions of fertility and sexuality have never been treated neutrally. They have always been highly charged – in myth and symbol, in art, in law and social custom. We should not delude ourselves that we have grown beyond this state of affairs. Abortion is inescapably an emotional issue because it is a "flash point," a meeting place of some of our most basic and contentious views of sexuality and reproduction.

It is possible that by projecting all the emotionalism of the abortion debate onto one side, we are missing something important. For the Right-to-Life position gives expression to some aspects of abortion that are shared by many people who don't necessarily think of themselves as Right-to-Lifers. There is a great "mushy middle" made up of people who have opted out of the abortion debate. Many of these are women who have had abortions themselves. Many others are the lovers, parents or friends of women who have had abortions. We need to ask *why* these people have opted out. Why don't they come out and take action to ensure the option that was available to them when they needed it continues to be available, to themselves and to others?

The answer to that question is, of course, a complicated one, and has at least as much to do with the nature of political movements and what motivates people to take part in them as it does with abortion. But there *is* something in the character of the abortion issue that explains why abortion continues to be a "hot" issue, why it does not just go away. For we can't fight back and demand our right to abortion or anything else unless we feel sure in our own minds that what we are demanding is just, is right, is our due. But for most people, even women who have had abortions (perhaps *especially* women who have had abortions), abortion doesn't elicit anything like such clarity. Nobody *likes* abortion. The right to have one cannot be fought for with the same zest as the right to equal pay or universal day care. And, for most women in our society, abortion is still a dark secret, a source of shame. British writer Eileen Fairweather explains,

> [W]omen in their thousands won't come flocking to our demos when so many have never even *talked* to anyone of their own experience .... we have a legacy of shame, secrecy, and often pain which goes so deep you can't even bear to think about it – much less fight *back*. [1]

In fact, what abortion inspires more than anything else is a profound ambivalence, which finds a particular expression in women. And when we look at the two poles of the abortion debate, we see also the two poles of our ambivalence expressed in an almost crystallized form. On the one hand, there is the pro-choice position, which is identified with feminism, with women's right to self-determination. On the other, there is the anti-choice position, which is largely identified with the traditional view of women as vessels, as mothers, as nurturers. In our espousal of abortion rights, feminists have spoken eloquently to the former. Our very rhetoric expresses our belief in our right to "control of our bodies, control of our lives." We project an image of strength, of self-affirmation. But in doing so, have we left something out? Is there a dimension of women's experience of abortion that we have not adequately addressed?

It is the hidden face of the abortion issue, this deep-rooted ambivalence, that we must look at squarely and integrate into our political stance if it is to reflect women's actual experience of abortion. It is a basic tenet of feminism, and a ground-breaking insight for all social revolutions, that the personal is political. What we *feel* matters just as much as what we *think*. What happens in our day-to-day lives has as much importance as what happens at political meetings or in the corridors of power. While we have acknowledged much of our ambivalence among ourselves, in the privacy of our kitchen table conversations, we have largely refrained from talking about it publicly, disturbed that it does not appear to jibe with our stated public position on abortion, and fearful of how our opponents might use it against us. But as Adrienne Rich argues, discounting our feelings and our experience in deference to some "correct line" is not what feminism is all about.

> It is crucial, however, in abortion as in every other experience (especially in the realm of sexuality and reproduction) that women take seriously the enterprise of finding out what we *do* feel, instead of accepting what we have been told we must feel.[2]

And indeed, in recent years a growing number of women, many long-time feminists and pro-choice activists among them, have been "coming out of the closet" to talk about their ambivalence and the complex web of feelings they have about abortion.

There is in all this a realization emerging that abortion hits us at the very core of our female socialization. With abortion, as with other areas of our reproductive lives, women are at a historical juncture, finding ourselves faced with new and unprecedented choices, choices for which our history and our conditioning have ill prepared us. Never before have women been able to exert control over our fertility to the extent that we now can. Effective birth control, sterilization and safe abortion offer us the possibility of real liberation from the destiny of our biology. But the very prospect of this liberation also brings us into conflict with our own view of ourselves as women in a patriarchal culture.

The theme of ambivalence runs right through the literature on abortion and women's accounts of abortion. The feelings they describe are strong, complex, often clearly contradictory, as these two women quoted in Linda Bird Francke's *The Ambivalence of Abortion* show:

> This time I couldn't help thinking it was a human being, a living being. If you asked me how I felt about abortion, I would say I was against it. I feel very hypocritical.
>
> I thought, I'm killing another human being, but then I'd remember that it wasn't even formed yet. I had two sides going in my mind against each other. But I'm glad for the most part I had the abortion.[3]

Often the language women use to describe their emotional state is remarkably similar: one of the women above describes herself as having "two sides going against each other"; another woman describes herself as "going in two directions;" still another says she feels "pulled apart." Sometimes these contradictory feelings centre around whether or not to have the abortion. But often it is not the choice itself that women feel conflicted about – they *know* they want to have one, or they feel that circumstances make the choice for them, and they do what they have to do. Usually it is the act of abortion and its implications that produce the ambivalence. As one woman put it, "the decision to have an abortion itself wasn't hard. It's hard reconciling the feelings after the decision."

Like no other dilemma that women face, abortion pits our desire to care for others, to protect others and avoid hurting them, into stark and seemingly irreconcilable conflict with our desire to protect and take care of ourselves, to act in our self-interest. This is the choice – self versus other – that women are faced with when contemplating abortion. And since all our upbringing, all our socialization, all the cultural messages we receive lean toward putting others' needs ahead of our own, toward nurturance rather than self-actualization, it is no wonder we approach the prospect of abortion with such profound ambivalence. For how can we be women and choose ourselves at the same time?

Our response to abortion has to do with much more than "patriarchal brainwashing." It is not simply a case of throwing off the shackles of our inculcated female guilt. Abortion involves a web of complex physical and psychological processes that themselves pull us in two directions at once. It involves our bodies, our emotions and our spirits in a way that engages us on many levels simultaneously, and that ensures that our response will be anything but simple.

There is, first, a self-protective mechanism at work with abortion, as there is with any bodily invasion. Though we may know on an intellectual level that early abortion is a safe, relatively straightforward surgical procedure with a minimal chance of complications, on a more gut level we harbour many fears about it. We are disturbed at the thought of a hard, foreign object being introduced into our bodies, tearing away at our insides. With any surgery we fear being harmed, temporarily or permanently, and our first instinct is to protect ourselves by avoiding it. And although most of the available medical evidence indicates that one or two abortions within a lifetime will not adversely affect fertility, women harbour fears that having an abortion will do precisely that. "Will I still be able to have children?" many women anxiously ask, and it is not uncommon for a woman who experiences difficulty in conceiving to attribute it to an earlier abortion. But our drive to protect ourselves from physical harm in the act of abortion comes starkly up against a different self-protective mechanism: the desire to expel the "invader," the unwanted, unchosen fetus, and thus to protect our personal and psychic integrity.

On a different physical level, abortion interrupts and abruptly terminates a number of processes that are all aimed at ensuring the continuation of pregnancy. Regardless of what our minds or our emotions tell us, our bodies want to stay pregnant, because they are programmed to ensure the reproduction of the species. The physical changes of even very early pregnancy are dramatic. Our periods cease, our breasts become larger and tender in preparation for breastfeeding, the opening into the womb, or cervix, becomes softer in preparation for delivery. The hormone of pregnancy, progesterone, is produced at high levels, and profoundly alters our body chemistry.

Another, related dimension of this phenomenon is the initiation of the bonding process. "Bonding" refers to the emotional connection between mother and child, which is thought to have biological as well as social roots. Researchers such as Marshall Klaus and John Kennell have posited that bonding results from a specific, programmed set of behaviours sparked by hormonal changes immediately after birth that ensures that a mother will want to stay with and nurture her child. According to psychiatrist Thomas Verny, author of *The Secret Life of the Unborn Child,* there is evidence to suggest that bonding begins well before birth, and is in fact a gradual, spontaneous process that develops throughout a pregnancy. This only confirms what many women believe intuitively. Certainly women who are willingly pregnant often feel an emotional connection, a conscious love and protectiveness for the fetus, sometimes very early in pregnancy. In the context of an unwanted pregnancy, of course, the notion of bonding is much more problematic. But it is an important aspect of our response to the fact of pregnancy, whether it is ultimately continued or terminated.

The effect of all these physical processes may well be to make us, on some level, "want" to continue a pregnancy. But this may come up against an even stronger desire, on a more conscious level, not to have this particular child at this particular time. This deep-seated drive toward life and its creation sometimes clashes painfully with our decision to abort.

A sense of identification with the fetus may also complicate our response to abortion. For some women (and men) this may be specific and conscious, and connected with the conditions under which we ourselves came into the world. One young woman quoted in Carol Gilligan's *In a Different Voice* was faced with an abortion, and had herself been "unwanted" and put up for adoption by her natural mother. This fact produced in her a sense of identity with the fetus that "gives me strange feelings" about having an abortion because "I could have been an abortion."[4] This sense of identification, though not conscious in most of us, is another aspect of the abortion decision that produces mixed feelings. We all start life as fetuses, and many of us wonder whether we, too, may have been in some way unwanted by our mothers. This kind of identification is fairly typical of children's and adolescents' response to abortion, and explains why they so often gravitate to the anti-abortion position.

The decision to have an abortion is far more emotionally complex than many of us had thought. The same appears to be true of the emotional aftermath of abortion. The medical view of the aftereffects of abortion has changed considerably over the years. In the fifties and sixties, a number of researchers, heavily influenced by classical psychoanalytic theory, claimed that women typically experienced profound emotional disturbance after an abortion. This was not surprising, since the prevailing Freudian bias encouraged the view that a woman's desire to avoid pregnancy and childbearing was a denial of her basic feminine nature. These studies had an additional bias, due to the fact that one of the only ways to obtain a legal abortion in those days was to be diagnosed as having a severe psychiatric disturbance. In recent years researchers have discarded the view that abortion is inevitably and universally traumatic for women, and have gravitated toward a much more benign view of the phenomenon. A review of the literature in the late seventies found "a growing recognition by investigators that ... the psychological consequences of abortion are not nearly as serious and painful as previously thought...."[5] The most recent Canadian study, carried out by researchers at Montreal's Concordia University between 1977 and 1979, confirmed that "abortion does not have negative consequences for the vast majority of women."[6] Most of these studies have found that when there is a strong emotional backlash after abortion, it is usually because of the circumstances surrounding the abortion rather than the abortion itself. One of the most frequent outcomes of abortion, for instance, is the breakup of the heterosexual relationship, and this, far more than the abortion, is likely to be the cause of depression and other emotional problems. In fact, as many researchers have pointed out, giving birth is much more likely than abortion to be associated with severe emotional aftereffects, in the form of post-partum depression.

Despite the prevalence of this view of abortion as less harmful than previously thought, another phenomenon has emerged in recent years. Therapists and abortion counsellors see an increasing number of women seeking help to deal with post-abortion grief. These women are not, for the most part, the same ones who fall apart after an abortion because their lovers left them. Nor do they tend to have had any severe emotional disorder before the abortion. Many of them are active feminists, women with well-thought-out positions on abortion who have the resources to get abortions under the best possible conditions. Usually they have had at least some emotional support from friends, lovers and family. These are the women who, according to researchers, should suffer the least trauma from abortion and who should make the easiest post-abortion adjustment. But despite this and their strong pro-choice sentiments, many women go through a period of mourning after an abortion that is very much like the grief experienced after the death of a loved one.

When the grieving hits, women usually feel surprised, caught off guard. One woman, "Heather," discussed her reaction to an abortion in an article in the Canadian magazine *Healthsharing*. She found herself "spiralling into a depression" shortly after her abortion:

> I didn't expect such an emotional experience, especially the grief. I felt guilty and ashamed that I was so upset. We don't talk about the grief and the angst because we're afraid the Right-to-Life will use it against us.... But still I felt betrayed that abortion was made to look like an easy decision, and it wasn't for me.[7]

Some women don't talk about their feelings because they are afraid they will meet misunderstanding and rejection from other women. As one put it, "There seemed to be this unspoken rule that a good feminist isn't supposed to grieve." Added to this is the fact that many women feel they are somehow not entitled to have any negative feelings because they *chose* to have an abortion. Said "Naomi," featured in the same *Healthsharing* article,

> The women I talked to weren't all that supportive of my feelings. In fact some of them were cruel, telling me not to be so upset. After all, I had chosen this. I was young. I could still have children later on.[8]

The grief experienced by women who choose abortion because, for whatever reasons, they do not want to have a child at that particular time is palpable and real. But because the abortion was freely chosen the grieving is usually mixed with other, more positive feelings like relief, and it rarely leads to any after-the-fact questioning of the decision. As Heather put it, "I had carefully weighed it all out. It was still the right decision at the time. But I still had to cry, to grieve the loss of this potential child, and the loss of my pregnant state."[9] It is important to distinguish between grief and regret in these cases. The Right-to-Life movement has seized upon the notion of post-abortion grief and has used it to argue that women regret their abortions later in their lives. But while many women may deeply regret having become unwillingly pregnant and having had to make the abortion decision, relatively few would reverse their decision or say they regret having had an abortion. There are, of course, some women who profoundly regret their abortions. They tend to be the ones who wished to continue their pregnancies but who felt they had no support to do so. Often such women have either been deserted by their lovers or coerced by them into having an abortion. It is this kind of sentiment that is behind the phenomenon of anti-abortion groups such as Women Exploited by Abortion, whose members speak out publicly against abortion and deliver emotional testimonials about the grief and guilt they feel about their own past abortions. One woman told a 1983 anti-abortion rally in Toronto that "I murdered my own child."[10] The abortion experience has no doubt been traumatic for these women, but their "exploitation" stems not from an abortion itself, but from the circumstances surrounding it.

Women who have abortions for predominantly medical reasons are another, somewhat special case. In situations where the pregnancy is terminated because of the mother's health, or because there is good reason to think that the fetus is abnormal, women do not usually feel they have "chosen" abortion in the same sense as women whose reasons are more personal and social ones. These women essentially *want* to carry through with their pregnancies, and feel that circumstances have thrust the abortion decision upon them. Their grief is often more severe, and is more akin to the grief experienced after miscarriage, which is also little acknowledged and understood in our society. In addition, their pregnancies are usually more advanced than those of other women seeking abortions. Since prenatal diagnostic techniques like amniocentesis can generally not be performed until after the first trimester, these women have to undergo second-trimester abortions, which tend to be much more physically and emotionally draining because they are painfully similar to labour and birth. Although the emotional aftermath of these abortions can be even more disabling, women who have undergone them generally meet with the same kind of uneasiness, the same well-intentioned dismissal of their feelings that other women encounter after abortion. Said one woman who had opted for abortion after amniocentesis,

> It was very hard to talk to anyone about it. When I did tell someone, it seemed they were either shocked or else they tried to tell me it was all for the best. No one understands that I miss that baby.[11]

Grief after an abortion does not go on indefinitely, of course. After the initial impact, which can be quite intense and last days or weeks, the grieving sometimes takes on a cyclical pattern, surfacing every month around the menstrual period, which serves as a painful reminder that the woman is no longer pregnant. Heather said, "Every time I got my period for the next seven months I would say 'I would have been four months pregnant,' then five, and so on."[12] Interestingly, many women report that the grieving process comes to a kind of natural end around what would have been the time of birth, about seven to eight months after a first trimester abortion. There is also the phenomenon of "anniversary reaction," in which some women experience a period of sadness in later years on the anniversary of either the abortion or the would-be birth. It is important to stress that post-abortion grief and anniversary reactions are *not* the same as the emotional disorders sometimes cited in the medical literature on abortion. In fact, they need to be accepted as a normal part of the abortion process, in much the same way as we accept grief and mourning after death. Not all women go through a grieving process, of course. Nor should they feel that they should, or that there is something wrong with them if they don't. But those who do, need support and acceptance of their feelings.

All this talk of grieving leads us to wonder: is abortion a no-win situation for women? Does nothing but pain and suffering await us afterwards? The answer is no. Although abortion can involve pain, much more than we had previously thought, for many women the experience also becomes an important transition, a learning and maturing process. This is well documented in the literature on abortion. One researcher found that "abortion is often reported to have been a positive maturational experience, a 'turning point' resulting in increased responsibility and awareness."[13] This of course does not mean that we seek out abortion as some kind of "growth experience," but that faced with the choice, we have an opportunity to grapple with some very basic issues, a process that can have a positive outcome if conditions are right. For abortion is a life-and-death dilemma, and it can precipitate a life crisis of a magnitude that few other events in our lives are able to do. But as we know, crisis can be strengthening as well as debilitating.

For women, the transition triggered by abortion often centres around the issue of self versus other. In confronting abortion, we are forced to make a choice between our own life and the life of another being, the fetus, between protecting ourselves and protecting another. A woman who participated in Gilligan's study put it this way:

> I think what confuses me is it is a choice of either hurting myself or hurting other people around me. What is more important? If there could be a happy medium, it would be fine, but there isn't. It is either hurting someone on this side or hurting myself.[14]

In a real sense, we are also forced to choose between two different views of what it means to be a woman in this society: the traditional feminine ideal of passivity and self-sacrifice, and the emerging model of female autonomy and self-determination. Choosing ourselves and our own needs, while it can be agonizing, can also spark the beginning of a new sense of self. Gilligan found that

> By provoking a confrontation with choice, the abortion crisis can become a very auspicious time.... other women, who arrive through this encounter with choice at a new understanding of relationships.... speak of their sense of "a new beginning," a chance to "take control of my life."[15]

Choosing ourselves is very hard for women, of course. It goes against all our conditioning, and it emerges in many women's accounts of their abortions as "selfishness," a negative quality. As Heather explained,

Saying "no" to children comes out in our guilt as "selfishness" rather than simply being able to say "no, not now," or maybe "never."[16]

But coming face to face with this "selfishness" and saying finally, "Yes, I choose myself" can be a transforming, empowering experience.

> Having an abortion was a way of gaining control, of saying "no" to fate. I wasn't just accepting what happens, I was saying a very profound *no*. I really held on to that. It gave me courage to continue with my decision.[17]

This is not to suggest that choosing oneself and choosing an abortion are synonymous. In fact, the opposite is often true. One pregnant teen told Gilligan,

> I was looking at it from my own sort of selfish needs, because I was lonely. Things weren't really going good for me, so I was looking at it that I could have a baby that I could take care of ... and that made me feel good.[18]

For this young woman, the abortion dilemma was a profoundly maturing experience, which brought her to the understanding that she had a responsibility to others besides herself. For her, the abortion choice prompted a transition from a childlike, egocentric self to a more mature sense of her own needs and goals in life.

The choice to have an abortion is not always synonymous with autonomy, growth and maturity, any more than the choice *not* to have an abortion is with passivity and immaturity. Abortion is a deeply personal choice involving many factors, many layers of feeling. Some of us have abortions and learn nothing about ourselves. Some of us have children and do likewise. But the confrontation with the abortion decision can be an opportunity for real growth and self-understanding, if we are able and willing to seize it.

What can we do to help other women work through their feelings about abortion? How can we help make it as positive an experience as it can be? Perhaps the most important thing we can do – as friends, as lovers, as relatives – is to *listen* to women, and allow them to give voice to their feelings, whatever they are, regardless of whether they fit with our notions of what they "ought" to feel. For most women, the talking-out process, the "speaking bitterness," is the single most important element in working through the abortion experience. Many of us, when confronted with grief or any kind of heavy emotion, avoid it, or dismiss it. We say, "Don't think about it, don't dwell on it" and think we are being sympathetic and consoling when we are in fact invalidating a person's feelings. What we don't realize is that grief need not be morbid, but can be a healing process. It is painful, but it allows us to come to terms with our experience, and to emerge whole again. And the consequences of suppressing grief, of not working through the emotions surrounding an abortion, are likely to be problematic later on. "Unfinished business" can surface again years later, often in other life crisis situations. Midwives report that unacknowledged feelings from previous abortions are a common occurrence during pregnancy, and they sometimes find that it can even impede the progress of a labour.

These are things we can do on a personal level. It is also crucial that the kind of counselling women seeking abortions receive reflects this process. A growing number of enlightened abortion counsellors are attempting to deal with the whole range of feelings and issues surrounding abortion. But they are a distinct minority. Most of what passes for abortion counselling in Canada consists of a prescription for birth control pills and an implicit or explicit warning not to become a "repeater." Said Naomi, "After the abortion, I felt like a trapped animal. It seemed that all that anyone else was interested in was what birth control was I going to use?"[19] In one Canadian study of abortion patients, only a little over one-third found anything positive to say about the counselling they received.[20] By and large, counselling is a procedure that women seeking abortions go through only because they have to. Active, supportive counselling is absolutely crucial before as well as after an abortion. Many women seeking abortions have been able to do a good deal of soul-searching privately and with friends, and are absolutely sure about their decision. But others are not so sure, even though they present themselves at an abortion referral service or hospital clinic. Some women seek abortions because they are pressured to do so by others, usually husbands, lovers or parents. Some women do so because, even if they have not been actively pressured, they fear that their lovers will leave them if they don't. Still others do not actually *want* to terminate the pregnancy, but seek to do so because their lives are in turmoil, they are poor, or they simply don't know what else to do. With abortion it is important not only to *have* the choice, but to clearly understand the choice we have made, or it may come back to haunt us later. Canadian sociologist Esther Greenglass found in her study of abortion that

> ... when a woman is pressured into having an abortion when she herself may be against it, or when she is uncertain about it, there is a strong possibility that she will have unfavourable or negative psychological reactions afterwards. [21]

One of the consequences of a failure to "complete" an abortion decision can be a replay of the same scenario in a subsequent pregnancy. In one study, a woman attributed a second abortion "to the fact that she never dealt with the first," and felt that, had she resolved the personal issues that led to her initial unwanted pregnancy, she might well have avoided the second altogether. [22] It may be that our society's failure to support women working through an abortion, rather than mere "carelessness" or "promiscuity," is often responsible for repeat abortions where birth control failure is not a factor.

This larger, deeper view of the abortion experience places some important demands, both political and personal, on us as feminists. As individuals we must accept and make space for these feelings, and create situations where we can help each other work them through. We also have to re-examine some of the ways in which we pose abortion as an issue, to take care that we are not invalidating or oversimplifying women's real experience of abortion. To begin to speak publicly about grief, about ambivalence in relation to abortion, is of course a risk. It threatens to divide us, to give ammunition to our opponents. But we have to trust that our increased openness will win us the support of many who are immobilized by their own ambivalence, or who feel that the feminist view of abortion does not speak to them or their experience. Finally, we have to ensure not only that abortion is accessible to women, but that it is provided in a supportive atmosphere that acknowledges all its depth and dimensions. The demand for woman-controlled clinics is a step in this direction, but we need to go even further. The final chapter of this book will explore some of these options in more detail.

CHAPTER THREE

MORALITY AND ABORTION

THE PRACTICE OF abortion has a long history, probably dating back to the very earliest human societies. Along with infanticide, abortion has been practised in all parts of the world, in many different cultural contexts. Anthropologist George Devereux found that abortion was extremely prevalent, though by no means universal, in the hundreds of primitive societies whose abortion practices he surveyed. Devereux also found great variation in attitudes toward abortion, and in the perception of abortion as a "moral" problem. In some societies, abortion was tolerated, but considered so serious an act that the fetus was buried with full ceremony. In others, abortion was treated matter-of-factly, with the products of conception unceremoniously disposed of. The more "advanced" societies of ancient Greece and Rome also accepted and freely practised abortion, with the full blessings of both Plato and Aristotle. According to social historian Linda Gordon, "almost all preindustrial societies accepted abortion."[1] But because of its attendant hazards, abortion was not the most common method of family limitation in most primitive cultures. Infanticide was in fact a safer (for the woman) and more reliable way of controlling the number of offspring, and it was also accepted, though not without anguish, as a practical necessity of life.

With the rise of Christianity abortion came to be seen in the Western world as a full-blown moral "problem." According to Simone de Beauvoir,

It was Christianity which revolutionized moral ideas in this matter
by endowing the embryo with a soul; for then abortion became a crime
against the fetus itself.[2]

The approach to the moral dilemma posed by abortion has thus been
heavily influenced by Christian moral philosophy, with its reliance on
Aristotelian logic and its adherence to "Divine Law" — a system of
universal moral principles thought to govern all human thought and
action. In the Western tradition of moral philosophy, there is a high
value placed on reason and "objectivity," and a corresponding distrust of emotion and subjectivity. Moral principles are arrived at
through a process of logical, deductive reasoning, which ideally
should not be sullied by personal feelings or considerations of one's
life circumstances.

With regard to abortion in particular, until relatively recently
Western moral philosophy has been almost exclusively concerned
with a single aspect of the abortion dilemma, namely the question of
"when life begins" and thus when abortion is or is not permissible.
Various cutoff points have been debated endlessly through the centuries. It is not well known, for example, that the Catholic Church has
not always considered abortion a sin. The medieval church followed
what is known as the "forty- and eighty-day rule," whereby the soul
was thought to enter the male fetus forty days after conception and the
female fetus eighty days after conception. Abortion of a male up to
forty days, and of a female up to eighty days, was considered permissible by the church. (What is not known, of course, is how the sex of the
fetus was to be determined. Presumably if one opted for abortion after
the first forty days, one took a chance that the fetus was not male,
because God, of course, *would* know.) In 1869 the Church officially
abandoned the forty- and eighty-day rule, and adopted the position
that the soul was infused at conception, which effectively outlawed all
abortions.

Other cutoff points have also been prevalent. The one most common throughout history has been "quickening," the point at which a
woman becomes aware of fetal movement, which occurs around the
fourth or fifth month of pregnancy. Abortion before quickening was
accepted by many primitive societies, and was recognized in English

common law until the nineteenth century. "Viability," the point at which the fetus is able to survive outside the womb, is the limit accepted by most modern-day proponents of abortion, and it formed the basis for the 1973 Supreme Court decision that legalized abortion in the U.S. American abortion activist-turned-opponent Bernard Nathanson has proposed implantation, the point at which the fertilized egg attaches itself to the wall of the uterus a few days after conception, as the cutoff point for abortion, in an effort to outlaw abortion while continuing to permit use of contraceptive methods like the IUD and the morning-after pill, which prevent implantation rather than conception. But in this he stands almost alone among both advocates and opponents of abortion.

Western moral thought on abortion has also been concerned with the related question of the "moral standing" of the fetus – whether or not it is a "person," with all the attendant rights of a human person. This discussion is viewed by most people within the context of the *legal* rights of the fetus. And indeed, U.S. and Canadian law currently hold that a fetus in the early stages of development is *not* a person. But ethicists are quick to point out that morality and law are two quite distinct systems, whose categories may overlap but are not synonymous. One may, in fact, take the stand that a fetus is not a person in the legal sense without disavowing all rights or moral status that the fetus may have. This is an important distinction, because this chapter will focus on moral, *not* legal categories when it discusses the various views of the "rights" of the fetus.

The moral standing of the fetus is a broader and more sophisticated concept than the simple notion of "when life begins," and it has increasingly dominated contemporary moral thought on abortion. It has formed the nub of the work of utilitarian theorists like L.W. Sumner and bioethicist Joseph Fletcher, who have used it to justify abortion in a variety of situations. The utilitarian theorists, who now constitute the mainstream of contemporary, non-Catholic moral philosophy, reject the concept of universal moral absolutes. But they still adhere to the Western tradition of deductive reasoning to arrive at moral principles. In fact, although much recent moral theory has aided efforts to make abortion more accessible to women and has helped remove the moral taint surrounding it, most of the discussion still takes place on an abstract plane utterly divorced from the life circumstances in which the abortion dilemma is situated. Moral philosophers are given to statements like "a fetus is a human being which is not yet a person," which probably strike the average person as a kind of semantic conundrum. To read some of the moral theory on abortion, in fact, is to be uncomfortably reminded of the old caricature of the Catholic theologians debating how many angels could dance on the head of a pin. One wants to cry out that there is a real woman involved here, facing a real dilemma, experiencing real anguish.

The problems inherent in the traditional Western philosophical approach to the morality of abortion are becoming more and more evident. We understand now more clearly than ever that "life" is a process, a continuum. It does not infuse itself at some magic moment. The difficulty of defining what an abortion is has been made infinitely more complex by the introduction of the IUD and the "morning-after pill," and the ongoing development of even newer contraceptives, which appear to function as very early abortifacients by preventing implantation rather than conception. The traditional cutoff points for abortion also no longer apply. Since we now know that fetuses exhibit movement well before the pregnant woman becomes aware of it, the whole notion of quickening has become obsolete, as has the concept of viability. New developments in medical technology have revolutionized childbirth to the extent that sophisticated life-support systems can now sustain fetuses as early as twenty weeks gestation and as small as five hundred grams. And this technology is rapidly being further refined, pushing the limits of viability further and further back toward conception. Viability is no longer a simple biological characteristic, but relative to the technology available at a given time and place. Thus, many fetuses that would not have been viable a few years ago are viable now, and, as Bernard Nathanson points out, "An infant could be 'viable' in New York City but not in a rural town, or in the rural town but not in Bangladesh."[3] And now, with the development of technology that can achieve fertilization and limited development of the embryo entirely outside the womb, "viability" is becoming increasingly irrelevant to the abortion debate. (Chapter Seven will explore the ramifications of the new reproductive technologies.) It appears that the moral theorists' efforts to keep pace with technological developments and their impact on the abortion question are doomed to failure if they continue to confine themselves to their current categories and methods. Technology has, for better or worse, irrevocably changed the terms of the abortion debate.

The feminist response to the idea of abortion as a moral problem has been an ambivalent one. Feminists and other progressives are traditionally uncomfortable with the whole notion of "morality." They view it as an essentially conservative, religious concept that has been used to bolster traditional modes of thinking and behaviour, and to undermine efforts at political and social change. Some pro-choice advocates deny that abortion is a moral issue at all. A favourite slogan for a time in the pro-choice movement was "Abortion is a health issue, not a moral issue." We have used this idea to argue that abortion should be treated in the same way as any other medical procedure and should not be controlled by criminal law. But by and large, feminists have not accepted the notion that abortion is the moral equivalent of a tonsillectomy. We sense there is more to it than that, but we have not known how to come to grips with it without giving ammunition to our opponents.

Some of us have dealt with the dilemma by adopting the "clump of tissue" argument, which is essentially a version of the "person" and "moral standing" arguments discussed earlier. In North America, the abortion reform movements of the sixties were greatly influenced by liberal humanism, which is based on libertarian ideals and which values science and rational thought. Humanists have no use for the Christian view of the fetus as having intrinsic worth, finding it a backward and "unscientific" idea, shrouded in mysticism. Henry Morgentaler, whose involvement in the humanist movement in the late sixties in Montreal preceded his emergence as an abortion activist, has been the most prominent proponent of the "clump of tissue" argument in the Canadian pro-choice movement. In his 1982 book, *Abortion and Contraception,* he states:

> It is much more consistent with our present-day knowledge to conclude that in the earliest days of a pregnancy we are not faced with a human being, but with a very primitive form of life which only has the

potential to become a human being. Thinking of a fertilized ovum or an embryo as a baby is contrary to all our knowledge: it is as if someone affirmed that an acorn was already an oak, a seed a rose, or a blueprint a house.[4]

In a 1983 interview Morgentaler expressed the liberal humanist view that ascribing any value to the fetus amounted to fanaticism: "If you think a fetus is a person you must be either a lunatic or blinded by religious dogma."[5]

Feminist writer Michele Landsberg, who has done some of the most hard-hitting writing on the abortion issue in Canada, has also used this line of argument in her *Toronto Star* columns:

> Let's get something straight. If a clump of living tissue is a human being, then an acorn is an oak tree and an egg is a chicken and the church would be giving names and funerals to every miscarried fetus.[6]

To the extent that feminists have felt that we needed a response to the view that the fetus has full moral standing from conception, the argument that the fetus is rather an undifferentiated mass of living tissue, with no intrinsic worth, has provided it. But many of us have become uncomfortable with this idea, particularly in recent years. One feminist who publicly expressed her ambivalence on the matter is the American writer Lindsy Van Gelder, who recounted her own experience of an unwanted pregnancy in a 1978 *Ms* magazine piece:

> I desperately wanted a feminist article, pamphlet, speech, *anything* that would let me have both the abortion and my own ambivalence.... I wanted to *deal* with the moral balance sheet of abortion, not to have to deny that one existed for me. Instead people kept telling me I was misguided, brainwashed by the patriarchy. They patiently explained that the fetus was just a bunch of cells.[7]

In general, though, the feminist tendency has been to sidestep the entire moral discussion of abortion, either because we didn't see it as relevant to our concerns or because, though we may have been uncomfortable with the "clump of tissue" argument, we couldn't see anything else that didn't pose a threat to our basic position that women must control their own bodies. Consequently, we have largely abdicated any role in the moral discussion of abortion, and Right-to-Life ideology has filled the vacuum. Presently, to most people, the

Right-to-Life movement is the only participant in the debate that *appears* to be concerned about the moral dimension of abortion. Their solution to the dilemma is, as we know, a very simple one: abortion is wrong. Abortion is murder. At its most extreme, Right-to-Life ideology views women as the murderers of their unborn children. Most people abhor the extremity of this view. But they do have a gut feeling that abortion *is* a moral issue, and they see no one but the Right-to-Life movement addressing it, however simplistically.

It is, of course, untrue that the moral dimension of abortion has been the exclusive concern of the Right-to-Life and its chief progenitor, the Roman Catholic Church. Judaism and the Protestant churches, for example, have been deeply involved in the debate and have also developed thoughtful, complex moral positions. But because their views are, for the most part, more equivocal and not so readily adaptable to slogans like "abortion is murder," "protect life" or even "abortion is a woman's right," they do not translate readily into the public, political discussion, which takes place mostly in the media and at demonstrations. Because of this the average person is much more aware of the polarities of the debate than of the continuum of opinion in between.

Feminists, too, have been concerned with the moral dimension of abortion, but in a distinctly different way from the moral philosophers and Right-to-Life. Rather than focussing on the question of the rights of the fetus to the exclusion of all the other factors involved in abortion, we have taken what we see as a broader view and set ourselves the task of helping other women who face the dilemma of unwanted childbearing. Indeed, this was our main motivation when, in the late sixties, we first became involved in the struggle for abortion reform. Prior to that time generations of women had risked their lives and health to obtain illegal abortions in Canada and in the U.S. Taking up the coathanger as our symbol, we vowed that no more women should die or become maimed or permanently sterile as a result of trying to get an abortion. This commitment to helping other women and relieving their anguish has remained one of the major moral impulses behind our continuing efforts to make abortion accessible to all women, and to ensure that abortion services are provided in a supportive atmosphere. In a real sense, then, *both* feminists and the Right-to-Life movement have approached abortion from a "moral" perspective. But the intense, seemingly irreconcilable polarization has occurred partly because our starting premises, our basic moral concerns, have not been the same. We have been talking apples – the rights and concerns of women – while they have been talking oranges – the rights and concerns of fetuses.

In our approach to abortion we have been motivated by what psychological theorist Carol Gilligan calls an "ethic of care," which resists the subordination of human needs and relationships to so-called "universal" principles of right and wrong. We have refused to be bound by abstract moral dictates and have let our actions be guided by our concern for other women in need and our conviction that we must not suffer for the very fact of being women.

Among the myths that have been handed down to us through centuries of patriarchy is the idea that women have a poorly developed moral sense because they are too subjective in their judgements, that they act according to the needs of individuals and circumstances rather than on general principles. Women's "inconsistency" around abortion has often been noted; it is said that they frequently believe that abortion is morally wrong but still have abortions themselves, that they justify their own or friends' abortions while still believing that abortion, in general, is wrong. This inconsistency has been taken as further proof of women's supposed moral inferiority. But Gilligan, in her recent study of moral development and abortion decision-making in women, turns this kind of thinking on its head. Women, she finds, do indeed tend to make moral choices in a way that is qualitatively different from the way most men do, and from the way that developmental theorists would have us believe is more highly developed. That is, women are more "subjective," more influenced by feelings in their choices. They are more reluctant to judge others or to accept blanket rules for all situations, and are far more likely to look at individual circumstances and how the lives of those involved will be affected by a particular action. This tendency of women is not the same as a simplistic moral relativism, however. In fact it is highly dialectical, and attempts to integrate the concept of the "rights" of others with what Gilligan calls "a feeling for the complexity and multifaceted character of real people and real situations."[8] In short,

gynecology and providing abortions altogether, and has thus, perhaps mercifully, put himself in a position where he need no longer deal with the complexities of real life that he grappled with in 1977.

Where, then, does all this talk of the morality of abortion lead us? If our focus on individual circumstances simply leads us back to where we started — affirming that each woman has the absolute right to choose abortion – is there any point in talking about "morality" at all? Should we simply persist in our longstanding mistrust of the whole notion of morality, dismissing it as a trap, a form of repressive social control that has no real relevance to our struggle to gain control of our bodies?

I think we risk making a great mistake if we do. Morality is a deeply meaningful concept for most people, one that we could not argue away even if we wanted to. What we need to do is get away from the idea of morality as a simple categorization of right and wrong. We need to reclaim morality in its positive sense, and see it as a way of ensuring that we are responsible in our actions, that we seriously consider their consequences, and that we take the needs and rights of others into account as well as our own. In this sense, "morality" need not be inherently repressive, but can be an important tool to help us live with each other and with the rest of the planet. We do need to acknowledge that abortion is a moral issue as well as a health issue and a political issue.

Can we conceive of such a thing as a "feminist morality" of abortion? What would it look like? At its root it would be characterized by the deep appreciation of the complexities of life, the refusal to polarize and adopt simplistic formulas, described by Gilligan as the great strength of women's moral development. It would not be a mere relativism that rejects wholesale the idea of general moral principles, or that cynically denies the possibility or necessity of moral choice because "everything is relative."

A true feminist morality would strive to root the traditional Western commitment to abstract principles of "right" and "wrong" in the firm ground of our tangible, day-to-day existence. It would begin by reaffirming one of the most basic principles of feminism, that women have the right to control our bodies and to choose when, how and whether we will have children. At the same time it would lead us to acknowledge that we are not each an island unto ourselves, that our rights and our choices exist in an intricate web of interdependence with others and with the rest of life. One of the inherent limitations of an ethics based solely on "rights" — whether it be the fetus's "right to life" or women's right to control our bodies — is that it is one-dimensional. It assumes that we are all, in some sense, atomized individuals with competing rights, rather than beings whose very existence is rooted in profound interconnections with each other. It is with this understanding of our interdependence that we can make the courageous leap of "letting in" the fetus, of rejecting the idea that it is simply a clump of cells, of taking it into our moral accounting and allowing it to make some claim on our attentions. Doing so does *not* inevitably lead us into the trap of concluding that the "rights" of the fetus outweigh our own, or that it is immoral for women to say "yes" to ourselves and "no" to carrying a particular fetus to term at a particular time. But it does lead us to look seriously at the whole question of fetal life. The "right of the fetus" may not be the only, or even the main consideration in the abortion issue, as anti-abortionists insist. But it is an aspect that demands to be addressed.

What does "letting in" the fetus consist of? Acknowledging that it is "life"? It is, unquestionably, at least as we might say any small, multicellular organism is alive. Is it "human"? It is in the genetic sense, at least, since it has the same chromosomal makeup as other humans. Is it "independent" life, as Right-to-Lifers often claim? This is, of course, a question that is impossible to answer unequivocally. It is certainly in the mother's body and part of it, but not in the same way that her own limbs or organs are, a situation that might more accurately be termed a state of interdependence. Does the fetus have consciousness? Again, this is impossible to answer definitively. Newborn babies were once widely considered to have no awareness because they could not talk or "think," but we know much differently now. Similarly, our knowledge of fetal life is growing and changing, and there are increasing suggestions that the fetus has a developing consciousness throughout gestation, experiences rudimentary emotions, responds to its environment, and even feels "pain," as some pro-lifers have claimed. We may choose to dismiss the whole area of fetal psychology as another repressive male construct, as feminist writer Andrea Dworkin does in her book *Right-Wing Women*. Or we may decide to take it into our accounting of abortion, and attempt to integrate it with our understanding.

Perhaps the central question regarding the fetus, in most people's minds, is whether it is a human being, a "person." It is important to stress again that we are not talking about *legal* definitions of personhood, which have a reality apart from everyday life and which, as we know, are relative and changeable. Until little over half a century ago, *women* were not persons under Canadian law. Ultimately we must admit that the "personhood" of the fetus is not something we can make ultimate, "objective" conclusions about, since it is so much a matter of semantics and interpretation. In a 1983 court challenge to Canada's abortion law, pro-life organizations spent large sums of money bringing in expert witnesses like French geneticist Jerome Lejeune in an attempt to "prove" scientifically that the fetus was a human person from conception. But, as ethical philosopher Daniel Callahan points out, we cannot look to science for the answers to these kinds of questions:

> Scientific evidence does not, as such, tell us when human life begins. The concept "human" is essentially philosophical, requiring both a philosophical and an ethical judgement. [13]

We inevitably lead ourselves up blind alleys if we focus on the rights or personhood of the fetus alone. But we must at least acknowledge it as a valid concern, one of many in our moral reckoning of abortion.

What this acknowledgement of the fetus leads us to is a profound taking of responsibility for our choices, for the fact that we have, with full consciousness, terminated life. This is most emphatically *not* the same as blaming ourselves or burdening ourselves with an unnecessary load of guilt. It means, as one feminist who experienced post-abortion grief put it, "not denying that there was something alive in you, and that you ended that process." Perhaps the complex, multilayered, ultimately paradoxical nature of this process of "letting in" the fetus and taking responsibility for abortion can be hinted at in this extended quote from a young abortion counsellor who found she could no longer accept the idea that aborted fetuses were "just jelly":

I just couldn't kid myself anymore and say there was nothing in the uterus, just a tiny speck.... I struggled with it a whole lot. Finally I had to reconcile myself – I really do believe this, but it is not an easy thing that you can say without emotions and maybe regret – that, yes, life is sacred, but the quality of life is also important, and it has to be the determining thing in this particular case.... I had to be able to say, "Yes, this is killing, there is no way around it, but I am willing to accept that...."[14]

Ultimately what we are talking about is an acknowledgement of the seriousness of abortion, an understanding that it is a choice that cannot be made lightly. The potential trap, of course, lies in defining what is a "serious" enough reason to have an abortion. Most Right-to-Lifers believe that only a threat to the life of the mother is sufficient justification, and they claim that most women seek abortions for essentially "trivial" reasons. But in our honest appraisal of our own and other women's lives, we know this is not the case. That we cannot cope with another child, that we are not ready for parenthood, that we cannot face raising a child without a partner, that we cannot afford a child, that our method of birth control failed, that we are the victims of rape, that we cannot bear the anguish of carrying a child to term and giving it up for adoption, that we cannot accept the responsibility of caring for a handicapped child – these are the reasons why we seek abortion in the vast majority of cases. Far from being trivial, they are dilemmas of great consequence that affect our ability to be who we are and to live our lives with any degree of control over our circumstances. If abortion is, as Bernard Nathanson has said, an "inexpressibly serious matter," so, too, are the life circumstances that lead us to choose it.

When we try to conceive of a morality of abortion consistent with our feminist consciousness, we return again and again to the inviolability of each person's choice, which must be respected even if we ourselves would act differently under the same circumstances. But we also do not want to propose an entirely private morality, in which the individual retreats into isolation and receives no input from outside herself or her immediate circle. When we discuss issues of morality we are attempting to define and clarify our collective values, and find ways that we can live in some degree of harmonious interdependence.

We may not reach anything approaching unanimity, and perhaps it is just as well that we do not. But it is the exercise of grappling with difficult questions and listening to each other's perspectives that is important in a society that strives to be truly ethical and caring.

For there *are* real moral dilemmas arising out of abortion, and we as feminists have a right as well as a responsibility to struggle with them. What do we feel, for instance, about abortion for the purpose of sex selection? Without surrendering our belief in the right to choose, do we not want to publicly question whether this is a proper use of that right? The practice of sex selection by abortion is going on right now, to a limited extent in the United States, and to a much greater extent in countries like India and China, where it fits in with government-sponsored population control measures, and where male children are much more highly valued and female infanticide is still sometimes practised. (There have been no reports of sex selection by abortion in Canada, and it would probably not be justifiable under the provisions of the Criminal Code.) The sex of the fetus can be determined after the fifteenth week of pregnancy through amniocentesis, which involves extracting a sample of amniotic fluid from the pregnant woman's abdomen. Amniocentesis and a variety of other prenatal diagnostic techniques have made it possible to detect a number of genetic abnormalities such as Down's syndrome well before birth, and this has created a host of new dilemmas. Some handicapped rights advocates have challenged the nearly universal assumption by medical experts that a woman "should" abort a defective fetus. This assumption, they say, questions their right to exist, and diminishes society's responsibility to accommodate and respect the handicapped. Again, without intruding upon the right of the woman to make what is nearly always a painful choice, feminists may want to join our voices with those who question whether abortion of an abnormal fetus should be automatic.

There are other, agonizing problems related to abortion. Should there be a cutoff point for abortion? What should it be? Should fetuses be given life-support assistance if they are aborted alive, as sometimes happens in the case of late second-trimester abortions? In fact, it is entirely possible in North American hospitals today to have two women, both around twenty-two weeks pregnant, delivering in adjoining rooms. One of the products of the labour would be called a baby and be hooked up to life-support equipment because the mother delivered prematurely. The other, which could be the exact same weight and gestational age as the first, would be called a fetus and disposed of, because the woman was having an abortion. These are wrenching dilemmas that few pro-choice advocates care to be faced with, and while they must be faced, it is worth pointing out, again and again, that it is the pro-choice position that ultimately will make such situations rare, by ensuring that all women have access to pregnancy diagnosis, good counselling and early abortion, eliminating the delays and roadblocks that create the need for such late abortions.

So our "feminist morality," while taking principled stands, continually refuses to make absolute judgements. Does this make it a contradiction in terms? Most emphatically not. It simply shows the inherently dialectical nature of truly human values, as opposed to abstract ones, in its groping toward a reconciliation of an ethic of rights with an ethic of responsibility and caring for others. In that sense, our morality cannot be tied up in a neat, predictable package, nor summed up in a single slogan like "Right-to-Life." That is its strength, and that is the challenge we face in putting it forward and integrating it into our feminist politics and practice.

CHAPTER FOUR

MEN AND ABORTION

WHILE SOME CRITICIZE feminists for ignoring the fetus in the abortion issue, others (often the same people) do so for ignoring men as well. And indeed, with our steady insistence that "abortion is a woman's right," we may sometimes forget, or appear to forget, that abortion always occurs in the context of sexual contact between a woman and a man. (Except, of course, in the rare case of an abortion where the pregnancy is the result of artificial insemination. Even then there is male involvement, but not *sexual* involvement.)

Often the man is no longer in the picture by the time the abortion takes place, or the woman has chosen not to tell the man that she is pregnant, or she may not even know for certain who the father is. But whether or not the man is present within the orbit of persons and events surrounding an abortion, the fact remains that men as a group are intimately and inextricably connected to abortion. Like making a baby, it takes two to create an unwanted pregnancy.

In dealing with abortion and other reproductive matters, feminists have gone a long way toward eradicating the sexist notion that unwanted pregnancy is the fault of the woman, a kind of punishment for sexual activity that men are not expected to share. But while fostering the notion that men should bear an equal share of responsibility in reproductive matters, feminists have been reluctant to accord them anything more than a minor role in reproductive decisions, especially where abortion is concerned. There are some perfectly good reasons for this. Women are the ones who bear children. Women are the ones, still, who are largely responsible for their care and nurturing. It is our bodies and our lives that are at issue, so the decisions must be ours as well. Besides, ample evidence over the centuries has shown us that we have been prudent not to accord men much say in reproductive matters, especially abortion, because on the whole they have not acquitted themselves well in this area.

The most common male response to unwanted pregnancy when it occurs outside of marriage has been to "take off," leaving the woman to bear the physical, the emotional and, often, the financial brunt of either having an abortion or carrying the pregnancy to term. Studies of abortion and its aftermath reveal that, more often than not, relationships do not survive an abortion: the majority of unmarried couples break up either before or soon after an abortion.[1] In many cases, of course, the breakup is at the instigation of the woman, or the decision is a mutual one. But the most frequent scenario is that the man terminates the relationship on being told of the pregnancy or shortly after the abortion, or he just gradually fades out of the picture. Male reluctance to accept responsibility in reproductive matters extends far beyond pregnancy and abortion, of course. The majority of men still regard the use of contraception as a woman's problem, for example. And men are increasingly disowning responsibility for their own biological children, as Barbara Ehrenreich demonstrates in her book *The Hearts of Men.* Over the past decade and a half men have begun to "take off" in unprecedented numbers, abandoning their traditional breadwinner roles, defaulting on support payments and leaving women to be the sole financial support of their children.

Often men take the opposite tack when confronted with an unplanned pregnancy: they stick around and demand that the woman not abort "their" child. This demand is rarely accompanied by an offer to raise and support the child, however. Personal accounts of abortion reveal this particular scenario with an astounding frequency: the man will say he is "against abortion" or forbid the woman to abort "his" child, without the slightest awareness of the responsibility that this position logically demands of him. A woman in one study even felt that her lover was "more logical and more correct" in his contention that "she should have the child and raise it without either his presence or his financial support."[2] Another, a fifteen-year-old, acceded to her boyfriend's wish not to "murder his child." But after she decided against having an abortion, he left her to raise the child alone and "ruined my life," she said.[3]

This extraordinary attitude stems from a number of factors. First, there is the simple fact that, for many men, making a woman pregnant is a proof of virility, and they are unable to think beyond that to the consequences. One recent study of male and female attitudes toward childbearing showed that men tend to view it as a kind of testament to their "immortality," rather than in terms of a personal relationship with a particular child, as women tend to do.[4] And, as we saw in the last chapter, men are more likely to take "principled" stands on moral issues without any regard for the human circumstances. Simone de Beauvoir notes that

> Men universally forbid abortion, but individually they accept it as a convenient solution of a problem; they are able to contradict themselves with careless cynicism.[5]

Even when men have supported our right to abortion, it has not always been for the best reasons. Since the late sixties, the Playboy Foundation has been one of the chief funding agencies for abortion reform efforts in the United States. As some feminists have pointed out, Playboy's support has much more to do with the fact that abortion makes women sexually available to men without the inconvenience of unwanted pregnancy than it has to do with any philosophical commitment to women's rights. In fact, in the hands of such an ideologue of sexism as Hugh Hefner, abortion does seem like another of those freedoms won by the so-called sexual revolution of the sixties and seventies that has, so far at least, benefited men much more than women. Widely available contraception and legal abortion have made it possible, for the first time in history, for women to have sex with men without the fear of unwanted childbearing. Whether women are actually enjoying the fruits of this new-found freedom and getting what they need from men is another matter altogether.

Of course, there are many individual men who do not fall into any of these categories – men who support their partners through an abortion, men who take their parenting responsibilities very seriously, men who believe that women, like men, have the right to control their own bodies. But on the whole, our reluctance to "let men in" on our reproductive decisions has been well-founded, because men as a *group* have always sought to wrest control of reproduction from women. In fact, as we shall see in Chapter Seven of this book, the whole history of the patriarchy is in one sense the story of this struggle by men to take control of reproduction and make it theirs. We see this in a variety of cultural practices, which are only now being called into question: the naming of children with the father's surname, the male medical control of childbirth, contraceptive technology and abortion.

Though feminism has never actually worked out a position on the role of men in abortion, in practice we have designated only one appropriate role for them, that of the "supportive man." In this scenario the man is to provide emotional support to a woman facing an unwanted pregnancy, and to help her carry out her choice, whatever it may be. In fostering this role we may give men the message, intentionally or not, that they should put aside whatever feelings or preferences they might have and just "be there" for the woman. Some progressive, "feminist" men, who are sympathetic to the goals of the women's movement and who in many cases actively work to support them, have particularly gravitated toward this role in their relationships with women. (A lot of other men are, of course, not so cooperative!) So, to a large extent, what we have encouraged in men is a passive, auxiliary role in abortion, allowing them to participate in a way that is helpful, but perhaps not, in some important sense, truly meaningful. Perhaps this is just what we want. Abortion is, after all, a woman's choice.

But there is a problem here. In every other area of reproduction we are encouraging just the opposite behaviour in men: we want them to take equal responsibility for contraception. We want them to be actively and intimately involved in every aspect of pregnancy, labour and delivery. And we want them to take an active, equal role in child care and parenting. We have fostered this trend toward greater male participation with some ambivalence, always remembering men's oft-demonstrated tendency to try to take control in reproductive and other matters. But in the end we recognize that we must do so if we want to eradicate coercive sex roles. By encouraging male participation in all aspects of reproduction and parenting we chip away at the notion that bearing and caring for children is woman's "natural" function in life, that woman's place is in the home, and man's is out in the world. We also make a true and equal partnership in childbearing and parenting a real possibility for women and men.

We have to acknowledge, then, that there is a grave inconsistency between our eagerness to involve men in all other aspects of reproduction and our unwillingness to allow them a similar role in abortion. This means we must acknowledge and validate men's role in the act of procreation. It really does take two. This isn't to suggest that men's and women's part in creating life are somehow equivalent, as some maintain. They obviously are not. Nature involves women in the reproductive process in a total physical and emotional way. We go through pregnancy, labour, birth, postpartum and breastfeeding, with all their attendant physical, hormonal and psychological changes. By contrast, nature does not even provide us with a sure way of verifying which man has fathered which child. But, if we are serious in our efforts to, in a sense, right nature's imbalance and make reproduction a truly joint effort, it behooves us to make more room for men in the abortion process, to allow them a meaningful role that acknowledges their part in procreation.

This stance poses, of course, a veritable minefield of problems, which we must traverse carefully if we are to maintain our hard-fought struggle for control of our bodies. The Right-to-Life movement has long argued for male involvement in abortion decisions – as long as the men involved are against abortion. On Father's Day, 1984, a group of anti-abortionists picketed a number of Toronto hospitals to dramatize their contention that men should have the right to veto abortions. Some of the participants interviewed used arguments that were uncomfortably close to the feminist view that reproduction should be a shared responsibility. Raising children "is not woman's work, it's humanity's work," said one man.[6] We should have no illusions about the fact that our arguments for greater male involvement can and will be used against us. This does not mean that we should reject them altogether, but only that we must be continually clarifying and strengthening our position.

Another pitfall lies in the fact that, to many men, "meaningful involvement" equals control. The only power they know is power over others. They do not understand how to participate in truly cooperative decision-making. As a rule women are much more schooled in the art of cooperation, of sharing power and encouraging others to offer input, whether we agree with it or not. So when we call for greater male involvement in abortion and other reproductive matters, we must do so with the regrettable understanding that many men, perhaps most men, are not yet capable of this kind of power-sharing, and we must act accordingly.

We can say that we support male involvement in abortion decisions, but, as always, life presents us with complex, unwieldy situations where hard-and-fast rules can't be applied. For example, if the man withdraws from the relationship as soon as he finds out about the pregnancy, there is no question of his continued involvement in the process – he has made his choice. But what about women who don't tell their partners they are pregnant, who simply go off and quietly have an abortion? Are we dictating to them that they must involve their partners? Obviously we cannot do so. Most often when a woman does this, she has good reason to believe that telling her lover about the pregnancy may have bad repercussions. She may fear that he will try to prevent her from having the abortion, or may actually physically harm her. It is an uncomfortable fact that pregnancy is one of the situations in which wife battering is most likely to occur, and some men have been known to respond to the news of an unwanted pregnancy with rage and violence because they feel "tricked" or blame the woman.

In the end we must come back to our starting point: abortion is still a woman's right, a woman's choice. This means that when push comes to shove, when a man and a woman cannot come to agreement, it is the woman's wishes that must prevail. We cannot allow men any kind of absolute veto over our abortion decisions. Further, we must fight any attempts to enshrine such a veto power in law. One such attempt occurred in Toronto in the spring of 1984, when a husband, Alexander Medhurst, tried to block his wife's abortion with a court injunction. Although his application was ultimately denied and the Supreme Court of Ontario ruled that the father of an unborn child has no legal right to prevent it from being aborted, Medhurst succeeded in delaying his wife's abortion by several weeks, causing her increased health risk and considerable anguish. We shall undoubtedly see more such cases: although Medhurst was not against abortion in principle and had no discernible ties to anti-abortion groups, pro-life organizations in the U.S. and Canada have taken a keen interest in such cases and have supported them financially and politically.

What about instances where the man agrees to take and raise the child himself? The woman's right to choose abortion should be no different in this situation than in any other, though it is hoped that she would give full and honest consideration to such an offer in making her decision. In fact, however, such instances are exceedingly rare. Although some men may voice such intentions during the pregnancy, few are able or willing to carry through on the commitment. Usually the men are simply not serious, or are deluding themselves in some way. Medhurst, for example, admitted to a reporter that his real hope in seeking to block his wife's abortion was that having the baby would heal his crumbling marriage.[7]

By the same token, we cannot allow men to force us into abortions we don't want. This happens more often than many people realize, not because men force women kicking and screaming into hospitals and abortion clinics, but because women's economic and emotional dependence on men can make them unable to carry out their own wishes. Forced abortion can have as devastating consequences for women as denied abortion. Naomi, whose own abortion is touched on in Chapter Two, gives this account of her hospital roommate:

> [The woman] was perhaps thirty, a recent immigrant to Canada. She had one child, and had been forced by her husband to have this abortion, her second in six months. She kept repeating that she wanted to die. She felt that she had killed her child. She had not been allowed a choice, and her anxiety was tremendous.[8]

How, then, can we create a greater space, a more substantive role in abortion decisions for men, without surrendering our legitimate right to control our own bodies? To begin with we have to go beyond the fairly one-dimensional notion of the "supportive man" and allow for a more complex process that acknowledges men's role in procreation.

An important part of this is acknowledging that men, too, have feelings about abortion. Their ambivalence has to be dealt with, their wishes have to be allowed expression and listened to, even if they are not agreeable to us, and even if we ultimately don't go along with them.

Just what is men's emotional response to abortion? It is a testament to the extent to which reproduction is seen as exclusively a woman's concern that there is such a dearth of literature on the subject. Roger Wade, a counsellor at a Colorado abortion clinic, has produced one of the few substantive resources on the subject. His booklet, *For Men About Abortion,* is based on his experience of counselling more than 1,200 men accompanying women to abortions. According to Wade, the first concern of most men is for the physical safety of their partners – as it is for women themselves. Any surgical procedure is accompanied by fears that some kind of harm will result. After that fear is assuaged, men exhibit a range of emotions as wide as women's. But there are some fairly typical responses. Men commonly adopt the role of the strong, silent protector, what Wade calls the "John Wayne" role. They may focus on the woman's emotional state while hiding their own feelings. Naomi described this reaction in her partner:

> Michael was very supportive. But he felt that he had to deny his own feelings in order to be there for me, which turned out to be a way of blocking his emotions.[9]

A variant of the John Wayne role that Wade identifies is the "jester" role, where the man tries to keep things light by making jokes and cheering his partner up. Men understandably gravitate to these kinds of roles because they are consistent with the male sex-role expectations of our society – men are tough, they don't give in to their emotions. It is, in a sense, safer for a man to play a role and thus keep his emotional distance from a painful situation, but by doing so he may be robbing himself of an important human experience as well as unfairly expecting his partner to shoulder the emotional burden for both of them.

Men sometimes, with the best of intentions, keep silent about their preference and withdraw from the abortion decision in the belief that it is "all up to her." This is true in a sense, but, Wade says, such a withdrawal can also be interpreted by the woman as a "Pontius Pilate" response, a disavowal of responsibility and an abandonment of her to the lonely process of soul-searching. Men also attempt to take on the whole responsibility for the pregnancy, berating themselves for "failing to protect their woman" and saying things like "*I* got you pregnant." Again, this kind of paternalistic response fits in with the prescribed male role, but is not very helpful for either party.

Like women, men may experience profound ambivalence and sadness surrounding an abortion. They may on one level want to continue with the pregnancy, even while knowing that to do so would be a grave mistake. They may also experience grief after the abortion, though often their grief is not simply for a child lost, but for a potential *son*. And men's failure to work through their feelings around an abortion can occasionally have devastating consequences. One man who did not make clear to his wife the strength of his desire that she carry through with the pregnancy suffered severe emotional repercussions. Even several years after the abortion he told writer Linda Bird Francke, "I'm still not sure I have buried that fetus."[10]

The feelings of the men quoted here and those counselled by Wade may not be typical: these are men who, after all, did *not* "take off," who were aware and committed enough to support their partners through the abortion process. But they do give a hint of the potential depth and breadth of male involvement in abortion and indeed the whole range of reproductive experiences. But as it stands now, men's needs are in no way being addressed in the way abortion services are provided in Canada. They are treated as largely peripheral to the whole process, when in fact their role is a central one, particularly as a strong source of emotional sharing and support for women. Some have suggested, in fact, that men's role in abortion is analogous to their growing role in the birth process. Once shut out there, too, men are now becoming deeply involved in their partners' labours and are physically present at their children's births. (Male presence at abortion procedures is, however, probably an idea whose time has not yet come. One progressive administrator at a U.S. abortion clinic began allowing men in the procedure room and claims that the fainting rate forced her to terminate the experiment almost immediately. Interestingly, this is precisely the same as the old objections to having men in hospital delivery rooms.) Counselling services and support groups, while scanty for women seeking abortion, are virtually non-existent for men. According to Wade, "Feeling excluded is the most frequently expressed complaint" of men involved in an abortion.[11] And it may be that by allowing so little space for men to explore their response to abortion, we are perpetuating the polarization between men and women around the issue. In the Medhurst case mentioned earlier, for example, it is possible that the husband would never have taken such extreme legal measures if his feelings about the decision had been properly acknowledged. He had been present at the birth of an earlier child, and his anguish over the loss of another was undeniably real. And he complained, with some bitterness, about the fact that nowhere in the process involving his wife, the doctors and the hospital abortion committee were his wishes taken into account.

Feminists should, with caution, re-assess our perspective on the male role in abortion. We should ask whether, by keeping men's role so circumscribed, we are actually discouraging them from real emotional involvement, and from a full sense of shared responsibility in reproduction. Women are now faced with agonizing, unprecedented choices. We should not have to make them alone.

CHAPTER FIVE

"CHOICE":
PURE AND SIMPLE?

IN THE MID-SEVENTIES the abortion rights movement in North America began to popularize the notion of "choice." This was not the result of any formal, theoretical shift, but was rather a spontaneous development that quickly took firm root in the rhetoric of the movement. It was nonetheless an important political and ideological change. Abortion rights, and, indeed, feminism itself, had come to be identified in the popular mind with an anti-family, anti-child mentality that had little respect for traditional values and cultural traditions. The opponents of feminism and abortion attempted to capitalize on this: feminists, they said, see children as mere inconveniences, obstacles to career fulfillment; pro-abortionists, they said, have no respect for the value of life and, even worse, want to impose their lack of values on the rest of society. In adopting the rhetoric of choice, abortion rights activists had a weapon to counteract that public perception. They were not saying that abortion was a good thing, or that anyone should have an abortion. They were simply arguing that each person had the right to decide, but not to impose his or her personal beliefs on others.

What the notion of choice did was to foster a new clarity in the abortion debate: it was not a question of being "pro"-abortion or "anti"-abortion, but of being for or against the right of the individual to choose and act accordingly. Choice also acknowledged the religious and cultural pluralism of North American society, and the diversity of opinion on the morality of abortion. And, perhaps most importantly, it allowed for a separation of personal values and public values. Women who had profound moral qualms about abortion, or who were strongly against abortion for themselves, were nonetheless able to embrace at least some of the abortion rights position if they believed, at the same time, that they had no right to dictate the actions of others. This is an important distinction which, for example, Italian women made by the thousands in the 1981 national referendum on abortion. Disregarding the Pope's expressed instructions, they voted against repealing the country's liberalized abortion law. At the time, many expressed the sentiment that, although they themselves were against abortion, they did not think it was the Pope's or anyone else's business to deny the option of abortion to others. In fact, many Catholics make this distinction, at least in private, much more readily than is commonly thought. Often, as in other aspects of abortion, a personal experience is the catalyst that brings the issue of choice to the fore, as it did for this Catholic woman, a close friend of Rosie Jimenez, whose death after a botched illegal abortion in 1977, following the cutoff of Medicaid funding for abortions, was widely publicized in the United States:

> I used to think that abortion is a mortal sin, but this experience with Rosie has changed me. Personally, I could not go through an abortion. I'm such a mother.... even if I were raped, I would raise whatever baby I had because it is part of me. That is my personal belief. But I can't say this is the right choice for everybody else. I don't have the right to tell someone else what they should or should not do. If you think you want an abortion, then you should have one. [1]

So the notion of choice has taken hold and, in fact, has become a kind of rhetorical shorthand for abortion rights. It is *the* slogan of the movement, and we see it in endless variations on buttons, leaflets, placards ("The Right to Choose," "Choice: Pure and Simple," "I'm Pro-Choice") and even in the title of this book. The opponents of abortion are particularly galled by the movement's pre-emption of the word, and many regard it merely as a "euphemism for murder."

As useful a concept as it is, and as valuable as it has been for the credibility of the movement, there are considerable limitations to the notion of choice where abortion is concerned. Most of these stem from the fact that the availability of legal abortion is but one of the factors that affect our childbearing. Most of the important influences on reproductive choice are more indirect, are part and parcel of the social and economic context in which we live. As one woman told Linda Bird Francke,

> I do think we have a right to choose whether or not to have children. But for many of us our class and economic background pretty much makes the choice for us. We don't really have the free choice to have children when we want them.[2]

It was poor and minority women who, in the late seventies, began to be critical of the "choice" orientation of the movement. The overriding emphasis on the choice to have or not have an abortion did not speak to the experience of most poor and minority women, they said. It did not address the fact that they were experiencing pressures quite different from the ones faced by the mainly white, middle-class women who dominated the abortion rights movement. Poor women were rather being encouraged, and in some cases actually coerced, to limit their childbearing and were serving as often unwilling targets for contraception and, especially, sterilization campaigns. While middle-class women were fighting for the right *not* to have children, poor and minority women were struggling for the right to *have* the children they wanted. In parts of the U.S., there were reports of women being sterilized without their consent or threatened with the loss of their welfare payments if they did not undergo the procedure. While for the most part the same kind of flagrant abuses did not occur in Canada, and forced sterilization never became the hot issue here that it did in the U.S., subtler forms of coercion were prevalent here. The federal government's own committee on the operation of the abortion law found in 1976 that less educated women were two to ten times more likely to be sterilized in conjunction with an abortion than educated women. The authors of the report acknowledged, cautiously, that pressure from physicians was a probable factor in the high rate of sterilization.[3] The issue of sterilization abuse brought a much broader understanding of how social, cultural and economic factors affect women's childbearing options. It became clear to many abortion rights activists that real reproductive choice meant much more than simply making abortion legal and accessible.

Economics and abortion are, in fact, deeply intertwined. Studies of abortion show that financial hardship is the reason most often cited by women seeking abortions. [4] Lack of money is rarely the *only* reason a woman seeks an abortion. Most women do so for a complex set of reasons, but money frequently is the paramount factor, the one that tips the scales in favour of abortion. This is especially true for low-income families and single women. The abortion rights movement has, since its earliest days, argued that poverty is one of the most compelling reasons why women must have access to safe, legal abortion, so that women who cannot *afford* a child will not be forced to have one.

The problem with this argument is that it is valid only if a woman seeks to end a pregnancy for reasons other than financial ones. If poverty is the reason she is terminating the pregnancy, if in fact she wants the child but cannot afford to have it, she is actually being coerced into an abortion. She does not, in fact, have a choice at all. For many women, this is precisely their perception of the situation: they go to abortion counsellors saying that they "have no choice," they "have to" have an abortion. In some hard-pressed communities in Canada the economic ups and downs are clearly reflected in the volume of abortion referrals: counsellors in Sudbury, Ontario, for instance, reported a sharp rise in the number of women seeking abortions immediately after the massive layoffs in the nickel industry in 1978.

Feminists should make our position clear that when we talk about the "right to choose," we are not talking about women having abortions solely because they can't afford a child. Obviously, if we are going to work for choice in our reproductive lives, we also have to work to bring about the conditions — social, economic, cultural — that will make it a real possibility.

The constraints on choice are not a matter of economics alone, but reflect a far deeper bias against parenting itself. Modern industrial society has isolated the childrearing role within the nuclear family. When people become parents in our society, they are expected to take on an enormous financial, emotional and physical burden, and to do so essentially alone. They are continually given the message that they are on their own, that they must not expect society to "take care of them." This is in marked contrast to most traditional societies, where the care and raising of children is treated as the responsibility of the group as a whole. In these cultures the family and the community are seen as interdependent rather than as isolated, antagonistic agents, and childrearing tasks are spread out through extensive kinship and social networks. In *Sex and Destiny,* Germaine Greer extensively documents her contention that traditional societies, in their own way, truly support and celebrate parenting, while our society, for all its idealization of the family and of motherhood, threatens to "crush all pride and dignity of child bearing."[5] And women suffer a particular kind of isolation and oppression within this system, as Jessie Bernard points out in *The Future of Motherhood.*

> The way we institutionalize motherhood in our society – assigning sole responsibility for child care to the mother, cutting her off from the easy help of others in an isolated household, requiring round-the-clock tender, loving care, and making such care her exclusive activity – is not only new and unique, but not even a good way for either women or – if we accept as a criterion the amount of maternal warmth shown – for children. It may, in fact, be the worst. It is as though we had selected the worst features of all the ways motherhood is structured around the world and combined them to produce our current design.[6]

Despite the efforts of a decade and a half of women's liberation, women are still expected to do the *real* work of parenting, to sacrifice our own work goals, our own personal needs, when we become mothers. We are still being forced to choose between motherhood and personhood, between having children and being full participants in the larger society. Like poor women pondering abortion, we don't seem to have much of a choice. For though our society is still "pronatalist," in the sense that it encourages childbearing by women and families as a social norm, it is paradoxically anti-natalist in the way it robs both women and men of real dignity, support and joy in the performance of the work of parenting.

In this context, many women may well be "choosing" abortion not because they do not, at heart, want children, but because their prospects as mothers are so bleak in this society. As Vicki Van Wagner, a Toronto midwife and childbirth educator, puts it:

In unchosen pregnancies, women may deeply regret that they are not in a situation which would allow them to raise a child.... For many women ... it is not clear that they don't *want* a child, it is clear only that they cannot raise a child in the situation our society puts women in.

The grief around abortion is a sorrow that we do not live in a world that supports mothers as human beings with lives to live beyond raising children. It is a sorrow that we do not live in a world that welcomes and cares for children, and values parenting. The pain comes from having to act out, and take responsibility for, *our society's rejection of children.*[7]

This attitude seems at first to run counter to our prevailing social mythology, which idealizes motherhood and children, but it is really the opposite side of the coin of that idealization. Our society provides very little in the way of tangible social support for families. Anthropologist and childbirth educator Sheila Kitzinger points out in *Women as Mothers* that Western society is organized according to the needs of industrial production and the labour force, not the needs of parents and children. This can be seen, for example, in current maternity leave policies. Paid maternity leave in Canada amounts to a paltry seventeen weeks for most working women. At the end of that time women are expected to suddenly return to work full-time despite the enormous adjustments of new parenthood, despite breastfeeding, despite their own and their babies' emotional needs. In this, as in so many other situations as mothers, women are put in an impossible bind, forced to make what are essentially no-win choices.

The lack of support for parenting manifests itself in a variety of other ways. Pregnant women are still expected to quit high-visibility jobs such as waitressing as soon as their pregnancy becomes obvious. There is a critical lack of high-quality, affordable child care in this country. The idea of fathers staying home with children is still considered little more than a joke, and paternity leave after childbirth is almost non-existent in Canada. Single women are almost assured of living in poverty if they become mothers. Unless they have exceptional social support networks, they face intolerable isolation and a draining physical and emotional toll. A new law passed in Nova Scotia in 1983 even disqualifies unwed teen mothers from receiving welfare benefits, effectively forcing them into either abortion or giving their babies up for adoption. It is little wonder that, given the prospects, so many women say "thanks, but no thanks" to parenthood, and opt for abortion.

Other societal biases that place constraints on reproductive choice have an effect on particular groups. For example, as we've seen, poor women — especially if they are members of visible minorities — are given the message that they should limit their childbearing to conform with the prevailing North American middle-class preference for small families. In some ways feminists have contributed to this attitude in our emphasis on childbearing and the family as a source of women's oppression. But childbearing and the family carry different values in different cultures. Many women quite simply do not want to limit their families to only one or two children, because they don't see it as an advantage to do so in the cultural context in which they live. Yet middle-class health professionals ignorant of this cultural context often try to convince them that their lives will be better if they have fewer children. This kind of class and cultural bias comes across in a variety of manifestations. Many health professionals, for instance, cannot make the critical distinction between an "unplanned" and an "unwanted" pregnancy. Because they have been trained in a system that emphasizes the rational, carefully calculated planning of family size and spacing of children, and because they share those values, they often assume that women facing an unplanned pregnancy would naturally choose to abort it. But as we know, fertility patterns do not generally follow such a controlled, rational progression, and it is not at all clear that it is even desirable that they should. Germaine Greer convincingly demonstrates that government-sponsored family planning programs are for the most part unwarranted bureaucratic intrusions into the cultural life of people who have developed their own values and practices around fertility. She argues that it is essential that we respect those values rather than arrogantly attempting to impose our own.

We have to recognize that many of the biases against childbearing in our culture have their roots in eugenic theories that discourage reproduction among the less "desirable" or "fit" members of society.

This eugenic bias is even clearer in the growing use of genetic screening and prenatal diagnosis in reproductive decision-making. Techniques like amniocentesis are indisputably valuable tools that can help us exercise real choice in childbearing if they are used properly. What is disturbing is the almost universal presumption on the part of the providers of these services that abortion is the only reasonable option for a woman who, for example, contracts German measles during her pregnancy, or who discovers through amniocentesis that she is carrying an abnormal fetus. More and more women, especially women over thirty-five, are being made to feel that it is a social duty to submit to these diagnostic interventions, and that they are somehow irresponsible if they do not agree to have them, or to have an abortion if the diagnosis is positive. Many medical experts argue for abortion in the case of Down's syndrome and other congenital defects on the basis of a kind of cost-benefit analysis in which the social and economic "cost" of maintaining the handicapped is seen as too great a drain on society's limited resources. Rarely do we hear the same people arguing for limitations on military spending because of "limited resources."

Advocates for the rights of disabled people have begun to be critical of this growing trend. They find that it questions their very right to exist and their "usefulness" to a society that values its members only as producers. By contributing to a climate of opinion that encourages the aborting of abnormal fetuses, society is increasingly excused from its obligation to make room for the physically and mentally disabled, to provide the kind of economic and social supports they need to live as full, participating members of the community.

Let us attempt, for a moment, to put ourselves in the place of disabled people faced with this kind of mentality. A Toronto woman, Susan Charney, is a victim of a congenital abnormality known as Turner's syndrome, which affects only women and which is characterized by shortened height, lack of sexual development and infertility. Charney is also an advocate for other women afflicted with the syndrome, and in that capacity she sometimes talks to women contemplating abortion after they discover they are carrying a fetus with Turner's. She tells of being visited by one woman whose first question to her was "Is my daughter going to be a monster?" "Did she think I looked like a monster?" was Charney's response to a reporter.[8] Another disabled woman interviewed by Gwyneth Matthews, author of *Voices from the Shadows: Women with Disabilities Speak Out*, felt personally threatened by the growing pressure for "automatic abortion" of defective fetuses:

> I think it reinforces the belief that a perfect child is *the* thing. If you don't have a perfect child, well, get rid of the disabled one now, and have a perfect one later.[9]

Matthews points out that while none of her interviewees were totally opposed to selective abortion, "most admitted to mixed feelings" about the prospect.

Raising this aspect of the abortion issue is in no way meant to question the right of individual women and couples to choose abortion if an abnormality is detected or even highly suspected. That is a difficult personal choice, which no group or individual who does not share the burden should presume to intrude upon. But the focus needs to be shifted from the question of whether or not these fetuses *should* be aborted, to creating the conditions for real choice in these situations. Feminist writer Rayna Rapp gives a moving account of her agonizing confrontation with the abortion dilemma after discovering via amniocentesis that she was carrying a fetus with Down's syndrome. Lack of support services for families of Down's syndrome children was, she says, a major factor in her and her partner's ultimate decision to abort.

> In a society where the state provides virtually no decent, humane services for the mentally retarded, how could we take responsibility for the future of our dependent Down syndrome child? In good conscience, we couldn't choose to raise a child who would become a ward of the state. The health care, schools, various therapies that Down syndrome children require are inadequately available, and horrendously expensive in America; no single family should have to shoulder all the burdens that a decent health and social policy may someday extend to physically and mentally disabled people. In the meantime, while struggling for such a society, we did not choose to bring a child into this world who could never grow up to take care of himself.[10]

Though there are more publicly supported services and facilities for Down's and other disabled children in Canada than in the U.S.,

Rapp's general point still holds. If the prospects for parenting generally in our society are disheartening, the prospects for parenting a handicapped child are almost unbearable to contemplate. Isolated, financially and emotionally drained, forced to fight for every inch of government subsidy and support, these parents and their children bear the stigma of being society's "failures" and must live out the consequences of our collective rejection of the less-than-perfect. Rapp also argues that changes are needed in the counselling procedures around selective abortion so that parents are not given only the negative side of what it is like to raise a handicapped child.

> "[I]nformed consent" to amniocentesis and selective abortion should include information about parents' groups of Down syndrome children, and social services available to them, not just the individual, medical diagnosis of the problem. [11]

Many of the constraints on choice, such as economic factors, are embedded in our social structure and can only be eradicated by wider social and economic change that creates conditions more amenable to having children. But others are matters of attitude, and are conveyed, as we have seen, in the biases of health care and social service providers. In recent years many of these biases have become exposed, and some of the more enlightened birth control and abortion counsellors have tried to provide alternatives. They have developed a more comprehensive approach to abortion decision-making, usually called "pregnancy options" counselling, which attempts to give full consideration to all the choices open to a woman and help her decide among them, insofar as her life circumstances allow her to. More than that, they try to offer some measure of active support to women in carrying out the various choices they make. If a single woman, for instance, wants to carry through with her pregnancy and keep her baby, they might refer her to a prenatal class as well as help her find ways of surviving financially. If she decides to give the baby up for adoption, they help her arrange that as well as give her the emotional support she needs to get through the experience. If she chooses to have an abortion, they can refer her to a doctor or clinic, allay her concerns about the procedure and, again, offer emotional support. Few places in Canada are genuinely able to carry out this kind of comprehensive approach because of the time, resources and sensitivity that it demands. But when it works, the pregnancy options approach goes beyond the implicit and explicit biases of most abortion counselling, and puts the responsibility for decision-making where it belongs, with the woman and, where appropriate, her partner.

In considering pregnancy options, adoption warrants particular mention. Adoption is considered by many in the anti-abortion movement as *the* solution to the problem of unwanted pregnancy. Yet adoption is no longer treated as a serious option by many counsellors working with abortion. This is partly a simple recognition of the fact that, now that much of the stigma of having a child out of wedlock has been removed, very few women choose to put their babies up for adoption. Carrying a pregnancy to term, going through labour and delivery only to give up a child is simply too wrenching a prospect for most women. Yet many Right-to-Lifers blithely propose it as an obvious solution, and they base their case on the declining availability of newborns for adoption. "There are thousands of couples just waiting to adopt your baby," they tell young single women, an argument that effectively makes the young women into baby factories for infertile couples, and ignores the fact that there is an *oversupply* of non-white and older children available for adoption. While sympathizing with their anguish, we can surely look to other and better solutions to the very real predicament of the infertile, some of which will be dealt with in Chapter Seven of this book.

There are other problems with adoption as a solution that have begun to surface in recent years. Although child welfare professionals have assumed that blood ties were relatively unimportant compared to social bonds and influences, an increasing number of adoptees are going to extraordinary lengths to search out and be reunited with their birth parents, and vice versa.

We should not let the problems with adoption and the simplistic way in which adoption has been pushed by the Right-to-Life movement lead us to dismiss it as a real option for women dealing with an unwanted pregnancy. For a minority of women for whom both abortion and raising a child are equally unthinkable, it will probably continue to be the best available course of action. Some changes have been taking place in adoption procedures in recent years that help make it, while still painful, a less emotionally wrenching experience. Until recently, for instance, women anticipating adoption were expected to ignore their pregnant state and were not allowed to see their babies after birth. Increasingly, maternity homes are encouraging young women to enjoy their pregnancies as much as possible. Adoption authorities are more amenable to practices that will allow the mothers to "say goodbye" to their babies – either holding them for a while after the birth or sending the adoptive parents letters to be read when the child grows up. We will help make choice more of a reality in abortion if we support these ways of humanizing the adoption process.

Despite its many limitations, choice is still a valid and powerful concept for the abortion rights movement. But we should be more straightforward than we have been about what those limitations are. The notion of choice is rooted in an ideology that views individuals and their rights as primary. But there are obviously limits to personal choice – not only in abortion but in a variety of other situations. If we uphold the primacy of personal choice in abortion, for instance, what do we do when that same argument is thrown back in our faces by the advocates of the "right" to read or view violent pornography? What is our reply to those who argue that they have the absolute "right" to choose the sex of their children, now that the technology to accomplish it is in place? All societies put some limits on individual freedom to maintain social cohesion, and the absolute personal freedom promised by the North American brand of liberal democracy is more mythical than real. In fact, the strategy of choice was adopted by the abortion rights movement partly because it was so consistent with this liberal ideology. The "right to choose" is an acceptable way of raising the abortion issue in a society that glorifies the individual at the expense of collective values.

We need a wider context in which to talk about abortion, and the more collective notion of reproductive rights provides it. A single-issue focus has long characterized both sides of the abortion debate. Although we know that in practical terms, we need to focus our energies on specific issues at specific times, it is not really possible to separate all the various aspects of our struggle, for they are intimately intertwined. We can no longer talk about "choice" in a vacuum. We must talk about the right to have as well as not have children, the right to control the conditions under which we will have or not have them, and the right to a social system that allows us at least some measure of real choice in reproductive matters. As Deirdre English puts it,

> A complete feminist reproductive politics must be a social and moral blueprint. It cannot end with the guarantee of the right to terminate a pregnancy; it must go on to include the right to have children, without supporting each child's existence at the sole expense of his or her mother. And that right cannot be separated from the rest of the feminist program of total equality. Reproductive rights must mean financial equality, so that women can raise children without being impoverished. There must be practical child-care support for working mothers and a complete turnabout in male responsibility for parenthood. Yet the individual right to have an abortion must remain at the heart of the feminist position. [12]

Making these important links puts our struggle in a different light. It becomes more and more difficult for our opponents to tar us with the brush of being "anti-child" and "anti-family," charges that have kept too many women from identifying with feminism and the pro-choice movement for too long.

As we look deeper and deeper into the notion of choice, we find it becomes anything but "pure and simple." The forces that work against our reproductive autonomy are many-faceted and growing, and they spring not only from the anti-abortion movement, but from some of our supposed "allies" as well, as we shall see in the next two chapters.

CHAPTER SIX

THE ANTI-ABORTION MOVEMENT

ITEM: IN NOVEMBER 1983, the *Toronto Star* published a letter by Lloyd Devlin of Williams Lake, British Columbia, that compared the Soviet attack on a Korean commercial jetliner earlier that year, in which several hundred people were killed, to the act of abortion:

> The baby, quite secure in its own environment, likely is unaware of the impending destruction facing it and has no way of pleading for its life.
>
> Imagine the terror and imagine the excruciating pain which the baby suffers as he is cut to pieces by a curette, or burned and poisoned by salt, or ripped apart by a vacuum, sucking him out of his environment, his pressurized "cabin." In hysterotomy he may even be gasping, and he may be struggling for life as he hits the garbage can. [1]

The *Star* ran the lengthy letter in a box at the top of the page and accompanied it with a photograph of a newborn baby. The letter elicited a highly emotional response, both positive and negative. Many respondents were appalled at the ugly, accusatory tone of the letter and the *Star*'s use of the photo of the baby. One of these letters came from a woman who had recently had an abortion, who said that Devlin's letter had "nearly broken" her and given her nightmares.

Item: In June 1983, a man tried to attack Dr. Henry Morgentaler with a pair of garden shears as Dr. Morgentaler approached the entrance of the new, illegal abortion clinic he had helped set up in Toronto. The following month, after the clinic had been shut down by a police raid, arsonists set fire to the building housing the clinic, virtually destroying the Toronto Women's Bookstore located on the first floor.

Item: In May 1984, Doris Anderson, head of the Canadian Abortion Rights Action League (CARAL), received an anonymous letter from someone threatening to kill her and all the honorary directors of the organization.

Firebombs, physical attacks, death threats, pregnant women called murderers: these are strange tactics for a movement whose motto is "Respect Life." The virulence, the hysteria, the sheer hatred of some of the anti-abortion movement's extreme tactics continue to astonish and disturb feminists and advocates of choice. Of course, the majority of anti-abortion sympathizers are not arsonists or would-be executioners, and dissociate themselves from such actions, which come from the fringes of the movement, or from psychologically disturbed individuals who may have no connection with it at all.

Incidents like these get a lot of media attention and feed our sense of outrage. But it is the more conventional, civilized tactics of the anti-choice movement that should arouse our deepest concerns, because they have more concrete political effects and in some cases directly affect the availability of abortion in this country. Hospital board take-overs, for example, have been the main political thrust of the anti-abortion movement in Canada during the past decade. Because the membership of most hospital corporations is open to the public, Right-to-Life groups have launched membership drives at target hospitals all across the country. In some cases they have succeeded in getting enough of their members elected to abolish therapeutic abortion committees and stop all abortions at those hospitals. This tactic had been particularly successful in the East, where the movement has effectively halted all abortions in Prince Edward Island, and very nearly so in New Brunswick and Newfoundland.

The personal harassment campaigns that anti-abortionists periodically launch against political and media figures they consider pro-abortion have perhaps even more disturbing, insidious effects. The most virulent of these was a vendetta against *Homemaker's*, a national, controlled-circulation women's magazine whose editor, Jane Gale, is a strong pro-choice advocate. In April of 1983 Campaign Life, the national anti-abortion lobby group, called for a boycott of all products advertised in the magazine and bombarded major advertisers — the lifeblood of a magazine like *Homemaker's* — with a high-pressure mail campaign. *Homemaker's* did lose some advertisers as a result of the boycott, but refused to knuckle under and appears to have weathered the storm relatively unscathed. The real danger of such tactics, according to Gale and other editors, is the spectre of journalistic self-censorship — writers avoiding the topic of abortion for fear that they will become a target of Right-to-Life smear campaigns. One Toronto journalist, *Globe and Mail* columnist Judith Finlayson, admitted that responses to some of her columns on abortion have given her pause. After one column appeared she received a flood of letters, some of which "made me fear for my safety," she said. "I am not avoiding writing about the topic. But you do take a deep breath before doing it again."[2]

Anti-abortion tactics are becoming ever more sophisticated. In parts of the U.S., anti-abortionists have taken to personal harassment of abortion patients and their families, whose names they are able to obtain from sympathizers who work in hospitals and abortion clinics. Some Right-to-Lifers in Canada and the U.S. have called for compulsory ultrasound examinations on all women seeking abortions, arguing that the sight of a fetus on an ultrasound screen promotes bonding, and that no woman would choose abortion after having one.

On no other feminist issue do we have such a clearly visible, upfront opponent as we do with abortion. Because the Right-to-Life's tactics are so extreme and highly charged, they often have the effect on us of waving a red flag at a bull, inciting us to rage and invective in return. One of the frequent effects of this dynamic is that it keeps us from examining our opposition coolly and dispassionately. Yet it is important that we begin to do so. Unless we can look at the anti-abortion movement with a clear eye and appraise it honestly, we fail to understand the strength and persistence of its complex emotional appeal. Without that understanding, we have no grasp of what we're up against and how to counter it.

The standard view of the anti-abortion movement among feminists, leftists and liberals is that it is essentially a conservative right-wing movement. Specifically, it is identified as being a major component of the "New Right," a term coined by the U.S. left to describe the latter-day alliance of the new "social" conservatives with the more traditional right-wing proponents of free enterprise and militarism. These social conservatives, typified by the Moral Majority movement in the U.S. and Renaissance International in Canada, see their chief task as the preservation of traditional sex mores and the nuclear family, and to that end they are in virulent opposition to feminism, homosexual rights and, of course, abortion. It has become popular to characterize the entire anti-abortion movement as New Rightist, and to point out the inconsistency of being against abortion but in favour of such traditional conservative causes as capital punishment, increases in military spending and opposition to gun controls.

When we stand back and look at the anti-abortion movement itself, we find that this wholesale New Right characterization doesn't entirely fit. While the New Right may be universally anti-abortion, it is not true to say that the anti-abortion movement is universally right-wing. This is not to deny the strength of the connection with the New Right, but only to point out that the two movements are not synonymous. Furthermore, there appear to be significant differences between the anti-abortion forces in the U.S. and those in Canada. In the U.S. the strong New Right involvement in the forefront of anti-abortion politics is clear, particularly since the ascendancy of Ronald Reagan. Andrew Merton's examination of the anti-abortion movement in the U.S., *Enemies of Choice,* documents the increasing predominance of the New Right mentality among the anti-abortion forces. But in Canada the link with the right is not always so obvious. The rise of a right-wing government in Saskatchewan in 1982, for example, has had a devastating impact on abortion access in that province. But in neighbouring Manitoba, it was a social democratic NDP government that raided and shut down the abortion clinic established by Henry Morgentaler in 1983 and charged him and other clinic staff with conspiracy to procure illegal abortions. The situation in Manitoba is complex, but one element of it is the fact that there, as in other provincial NDPs, there is a significant anti-abortion faction, made up of people who see no contradiction between a generally leftist orientation and their opposition to abortion. Manitoba health minister Larry Desjardins, for example, who strongly opposed the Morgentaler clinic, comes from a heavily Catholic riding with many anti-abortion constituents. The whole abortion issue has been a deeply divisive one within the Manitoba NDP, as it has in other provincial NDPs.

Complicating the picture is the pre-eminence of the Roman Catholic Church in the anti-abortion movement. While the Church wholeheartedly embraces the agenda of New Right social conservatives in the areas of sexual freedom and women's rights, there are at the same time strongly progressive elements within the Church, especially in the areas of peace and social justice. Many progressive Catholics are in the forefront of anti-nuclear and Third World solidarity movements, for instance, and many of them share the Church's opposition to abortion, seeing this stance as wholly consistent with their overall political orientation. All in all, we have to acknowledge that the anti-abortion movement is not the monolith we have pictured it as. In fact, it is a diverse movement of people who, in many cases, have little in common except their opposition to abortion. As Andrew Merton points out, the anti-abortion movement has its own political spectrum of views, its own "liberal" and "conservative" wings, just as other movements do.

More disquieting, for feminists, is the painful fact that the anti-abortion movement is largely a *women's* movement. We have sometimes fostered the idea that it is men who want to deny us the right to abortion, that the anti-abortion movement is yet another instrument of male domination. In fact it is women who make up the rank-and-file of the movement, women who do the bulk of the telephone-answering and envelope-stuffing that keeps anti-abortion organizations going (as, indeed, women do elsewhere). And while a good part of the leadership in these organizations is male, women are also well represented in the hierarchy, especially in Canada. Why is this so? What is the appeal of the anti-abortion movement for women? What motivates them to become involved in a cause that appears (to us) to go against their self-interest?

A large part of that appeal is precisely the "pro-family," conservative social agenda that predominates in the movement. The attraction of social conservatism for women has been explored by a number of American feminist writers, among them Barbara Ehrenreich, Deirdre English and Andrea Dworkin. They argue strongly against writing off these women as simply deluded or brainwashed by patriarchal ideology. And they all conclude that what lies at the heart of much of women's right-wing allegiance is *fear,* a fear of losing what little social and economic security they now have. English contends that women on the right do have their own self-interest at heart:

> The antifeminist woman is, like all other women, grappling with the weight of her oppression. She is responding to social circumstances – a worsening economy, a lack of aid and commitment from men – which feminists did not create and from which feminists also feel the consequences. The issues that she faces are the issues that face us, too: her fears are nothing less than our fears. The difference lies in our strategies for dealing with all this. Her strategy is defensive: reactionary in the sense of reacting to change with the desire to return to the supposedly simple solutions of the past.[3]

Involvement in right-wing groups also has more tangible benefits for women. English wryly notes, "the antiabortion movement accomplishes two things at once for these women: it defends their role as women in the home, and it gets them out of the house."

Right-wing anti-feminism arose in distinctly Canadian form with the formation in early 1984 of REAL (Realistic Equal Active for Life) Women, an organization proclaiming its intention to "defend the family" from the undermining onslaughts of feminists. REAL Women has attempted to focus its public profile on issues like equal pay and housewives' pensions, but what has kept coming up is its not-so-hidden agenda on abortion. Its legal counsel, for example, is prominent pro-lifer Gwen Landolt. On one daytime radio program REAL president Grace Petrasek was asked by longtime feminist Laura Sabia why she refused to work with feminists on some common-ground issues. "If you were against abortion, we might be able to," was Petrasek's heated reply.[4]

Abortion is central to these women's concerns, partly because of their general sexual conservatism and their belief that "bad," "promiscuous" women are the ones who seek abortions. But even more, they fear abortion because it has the potential to weaken one of the few binding holds that women have on men. As Barbara Ehrenreich says,

"To antifeminists who focus on the issue of abortion, it is the possibility of sex without babies that has undermined male responsibility."[5] Andrea Dworkin puts it more bluntly.

> Right-wing women accuse feminists of hypocrisy and cruelty in advocating legal abortion because, as they see it, legal abortion makes them accessible fucks without consequence to men. In their view, pregnancy is the only consequence of sex that makes men accountable to women for what men do to women.[6]

At heart, the anti-feminists harbour a far more profound distrust of men than feminists do. They also share a corresponding, rather sad conviction that women are incapable of developing their own power in the world, that they are inevitably dependent on male whim and preference for their tenuous security in life.

The appeal of social conservatism and the anti-abortion movement to women is understandable when viewed in this light. But it does not entirely explain their opposition to abortion. There is another element that is, for lack of a better word, decidedly altruistic in women's involvement in the anti-abortion movement. It is part of our conditioning as women (and, some would argue, our intrinsic makeup) to be nurturers, to protect what is weak and vulnerable – and what is more vulnerable than a fetus? At the heart of many women's opposition to abortion is a heartfelt conviction that they must act to protect those who cannot protect themselves, and they often make the connection between this and other acts of caring and social advocacy. Of four women anti-abortion activists profiled in Merton's *Enemies of Choice,* all make some connection between abortion and other social issues. One, Loretto Wagner, was an early advocate of the civil rights movement in the U.S. Another, Nellie Gray, compares the modern-day status of fetuses to black slaves in the nineteenth century and the Jews under Hitler. And Dr. Mildred Jefferson, a black woman, connects abortion with black genocide in the U.S. and "a class war against the poor."[7]

Some of these same themes are echoed by Canadian anti-abortion activists. One, Denyse Handler, publisher of the anti-abortion magazine *The Human,* calls herself a feminist. Another, Martha Crean, is also a feminist, anti-nuclear activist and member of the NDP. She sees her involvement with abortion as a reflection of her commitment to peace and non-violence and traces it back to her opposition to the Vietnam war in the early seventies.

> I'd go to an anti-Viet Nam involvement rally, for instance, and see that some were putting emphasis on abortion. If you wanted to be a feminist, you'd have to be for abortion. This seemed inconsistent, to support an act of violence rather than an act of peace.[8]

Crean's comments give rise to a question that has never been seriously debated by the women's movement: can a woman be both a feminist and anti-choice on abortion? Clearly there are many women who are both feminists and personally opposed to abortion for themselves. But what we are talking about here is the possibility of being a feminist opposed to the right of abortion for others, as Crean is. The question cannot be answered, of course, without asking another, more fundamental question: what is feminism? This is not the place to digress into such a theoretical discussion, but it is worth pointing out that feminism is growing more diverse, is developing more "schools" of thought, than ever before. It would have been much easier to come up with a comprehensive definition of feminism in the early seventies than it is now. Still, to the vast majority of feminists, abortion is a bedrock issue. By some, indeed, it is viewed as the foundation of feminism itself. No less a feminist than Simone de Beauvoir recently affirmed her belief that freedom for women "began with the womb":

> I have not stopped fighting for the essential feminist message – the right of abortion.[9]

Yet there are others who, like Crean, see abortion as an act of violence and thus completely incompatible with their idea of feminism, which stresses caring and non-violence. How, then, can these women be in the same women's movement? Is there room within feminism for basic disagreement on such fundamental issues as abortion? These are questions we may have to come to grips with. Of even greater significance for the pro-choice movement is the question of what to do about people in the anti-abortion movement who sincerely consider themselves feminists and progressives. The right-wing social agenda clearly does not apply to them. We can simply write them off as unrepresentative, a fringe minority, which they clearly are. Or we can go a few steps further and try to discover what lies at the root of their commitment, and why, on this issue, their sentiments veer off so sharply from our own.

We begin to find some clues as we examine some of the other issues in which Right-to-Lifers have become active in recent years. For many in the anti-abortion movement, the "right to life" refers to much more than fetuses. The movement is expanding its focus from abortion to other bioethical issues like euthanasia, genetic engineering and the rights of the handicapped and aged to medical treatment. The most telling evidence of this shift was their high-profile involvement in the sensational "Baby Doe" cases in the U.S. Both "Baby Doe" and "Baby Jane Doe" were infants born with multiple defects whose parents denied consent to surgery that might have corrected some of the babies' problems and prolonged their lives. Right-to-Life groups became active and vocal in both cases, demanding that the government intervene and order treatment against the wishes of the parents. The incidents generated intense debate over the prognosis for the infants: was the extent of their disabilities — chiefly Down's syndrome and spina bifida, respectively — being overplayed by the doctors who advised the parents? Did the parents' "right to privacy" in their decision override the infants' right to treatment? Response to the issue crisscrossed traditional political lines. One U.S. feminist and disabled activist, Anne Finger, was highly critical of fellow leftists and feminists

> who seem quick to take a knee-jerk stand in opposition to right-wing and anti-abortion forces, without considering it from the perspective of a disabled person or investigating the role that our community has played in this fight. [10]

Finger clearly linked the issue with the larger struggle of disabled people to participate fully in society, and said it was imperative, in her view, that "disabled infants have the same access to medical care as non-disabled infants."

There has been some debate within the Right-to-Life movement over the wisdom of extending the focus to other issues besides abortion. There are many who believe the movement should "stick to abortion" because it is the central "life" issue. But the voices in favour of a broader perspective, though a minority, are growing. In Canada, Right-to-Life groups have also begun to be active in these issues, and were quite vocal in the case of a severely handicapped Edmonton newborn who was given a morphine overdose by a doctor in 1983. They were also involved in the case of Stephen Dawson, a six-year-old handicapped British Columbia boy whose parents refused consent to an operation that would have prolonged his life. As a result of the pressure, the B.C. Department of Human Services and the courts intervened, overriding the parents' decision and ordering the operation.

It is beyond the scope of this book to delve into the pros and cons of these and other complex bioethical debates, which are becoming more and more common with medical technology of ever-increasing sophistication. These debates in many ways transcend our accustomed moral and political categories precisely because they are in some cases the creation of sophisticated medical technology and unprecedented in human history. They nevertheless have to be grappled with, and there is a growing consensus that, at the very least, they must not be left to medical experts to decide alone. Until recently pro-choice and progressive people have tended to scoff at the connection made by the anti-abortion movement between these issues and abortion. This connection is part of the Right-to-Life "thin edge of the wedge" or "Pandora's box" argument that to allow abortion cheapens the value of human life and opens the door to active mercy-killing, infanticide and a general readiness to dispose of "unproductive" or "undesirable" elements in society. This connection is becoming more and more a feature of anti-abortion propaganda, as witness a poster which caused some heated controversy in Kitchener, Ontario, in 1983. The poster, which was carried on Kitchener's public transit system, pictured a stack of building blocks with a hand ready to pull a rope tied around the lowest block. The blocks pictured an eighteen-week-old fetus, a boy with Down's syndrome, a person in a wheelchair, a senior citizen and a group of people walking. The caption read, "Abortion – all our lives are on the line."

What is interesting about this approach is that, however manipulative and oversimplistic, it does not really spring from the same anti-sexual, social conservative agenda that forms the foundation for much of the anti-abortion movement. There are different impulses at work here, which seem to stem from a genuine fear that the value of human life is being eroded, that it is losing the intrinsic worth it once had. This view is essentially a misplaced nostalgia for a time that never existed. In Western society, at least, there is every evidence that infanticide and maltreatment of the handicapped and other people considered deviant was far more common in the past than it is today. Yet the concern about the expendability of human beings is an urgent one in a capitalist/consumer society that views human beings solely in terms of their productivity and their ability to function in the marketplace. In such a society, it follows that those who are considered a "drain on resources," such as the elderly and the retarded, are considered to be of less value, and are treated accordingly.

Part of the appeal of Right-to-Life ideology, in its broader sense, lies in its giving expression to this fear, this sense that people have become things, objects to be manipulated or discarded for convenience. And it is Right-to-Life's advocacy of this view that has led to increasing alliances with disabled rights groups on particular issues such as the Baby Doe and Stephen Dawson cases. Many of these groups do not share the anti-abortion stance of Right-to-Life, but do not see that as a barrier to cooperation on issues of common concern. In fact it was a coalition of disability advocacy organizations and pro-life groups that was largely responsible for the B.C. government's intervention in the Stephen Dawson case. If we continue what Anne Finger rightly calls our "knee-jerk" response of dismissal and hostility to *any* issue that the Right-to-Life supports, we run the grave risk of alienating many – the disabled, the elderly – with whom we should rightfully be marching side by side.

Unfortunately, the *idea* of "life" abstracted from the everyday realities of life plagues the Right-to-Life movement's approach to these issues as it does their stance on abortion. It leads them to a simplistic "life at any cost" position that overlooks the quality of the life as it is experienced by the person living it. The elderly and the severely handicapped have less to fear from "mercy killing," for instance, than they do from institutionalization, which in many cases is a kind of slow death in itself. "Quality of life" has a hollow ring when it is mouthed by health professionals who view it as a fixed potential in a person's life that society has no obligation to try to change or improve. Quality of life is, nevertheless, a legitimate aspect of discussion on these issues, but Right-to-Life dismisses it as a mere euphemism for euthanasia. Somewhat ironically, the "life at any cost" stance has led some pro-lifers into a totally uncritical view of high-technology medicine and the desirability of using it in all circumstances. At its extreme, this enthusiasm for medical technology has led some Right-to-Life advocates in the U.S. to campaign for the use of prostaglandin injections for late abortions because this method is more likely to result in the expulsion of a live fetus than is the more common saline injection or dilation and extraction (D and E) procedure. They argue that if the abortion results in a live fetus, heroic, high-tech measures should be instituted to keep it alive. The warped thinking behind such a stance is almost breathtaking.

Nevertheless, the Right-to-Life movement is working at the cutting edge of bioethical issues that feminists and progressives have barely begun to address, issues that will increasingly dominate the politics of the rest of the twentieth century and beyond. Their solutions are for the most part wrong-headed and simplistic, but they are asking what is to many minds the right question: is life of value in itself? For it is not much of a leap from that abstract question to: "is *my* life of any value?" And that connection is made explicitly in anti-abortion literature and in media images such as the Kitchener, Ontario, poster mentioned earlier: if "they" can discard unborn children, maybe even handicapped infants and old people, what's to stop them from discarding you or me? In a society where feelings of worthlessness and powerlessness are epidemic, such an approach has a powerful, if largely unconscious, appeal. Of course, most of us know, rationally, that we are not in danger of being "liquidated," but the sense of identification is there nonetheless. They – the fetuses, the handicapped babies and old people – are "non-persons," and so am I.

What Right-to-Life ideology does so effectively is embrace all the most "disposable" elements of society and validate them. To the elderly, to the disabled, to the fetus, it says, "You are worthwhile, for yourself alone." Ethicist Daniel Callahan, who does not share the

Right-to-Life stance on abortion, nevertheless sees an important value in its position.

> The great strength of the movement against abortion is that it seeks to protect one defenseless category of human or potentially human life; furthermore, it strives to resist the introduction into society of forms of value judgements that would discriminate among the worth of individual lives. In almost any other civil rights context, the cogency of this line of reasoning would be quickly respected.[11]

The appeal of the anti-abortion movement is powerful and complex, but on every level it speaks to genuine fears – fear of change, fear of liberated sexuality, fear of ambiguity and complexity, fear that life has no value, fear of female autonomy. As a movement, it shows no sign of fading away. Although it has been and still remains largely a fringe phenomenon, it has always had an impact beyond its numbers precisely because of its altruistic, "guardian of the fetus" stance. Most people in our society don't go to anti-abortion rallies (or pro-choice rallies, for that matter), but many have nagging doubts about abortion. For these people the Right-to-Life may serve as a kind of conscience, a reference group of individuals who are seen as having their "hearts in the right place" and who are "not afraid to stand up for what they believe in."

How can we respond effectively to such a complex phenomenon? Clearly, we must take the fears that are crystallized in the Right-to-Life position seriously, and make an attempt to get inside the minds of those who experience them. We need to stop dismissing and objectifying the movement or we will not gain any understanding of its powerful appeal, particularly to other women. Up to now our stance has been entirely confrontational. We have committed ourselves to the political defeat of the Right-to-Life, and to a large extent that has been and remains our most important strategy. For we have no illusions about the fact that the New Right is just as strongly committed to wiping out all the gains of feminism, along with the rights of gays and lesbians, the poor and visible minorities. We have no choice: we have to fight and we have to win. But there are levels at which the confrontation mentality may not work because, as this chapter has tried to show, there are elements of the Right-to-Life stance that are progressive, or potentially so. Is it possible that we might join forces on some issues such as disabled people's rights? Is it even possible that we might disarm some of the more thoughtful Right-to-Lifers by showing them that our commitment to life, to the rights and dignity of human beings, is as passionate and as sacred as theirs? A reconciliation with some segments of the pro-life movement is unlikely, but it is a possibility to which we in the pro-choice movement should remain open.

CHAPTER SEVEN

CONTROLLING REPRODUCTION

THE RIGHT-TO-LIFE movement continues to do all in its power to deny women the right to abortion, and most pro-choice supporters blame the actions of pro-life groups for the decreasing availability of abortion. But in an article published in the Canadian leftist journal *This Magazine* in the spring of 1983, feminist writer Susan G. Cole makes the provocative argument that doctors, not Right-to-Lifers, are the real obstacles to abortion rights in this country. The anti-abortion movement, she says,

> ... has had a far greater impact on abortion policy than its numbers warrant. Mythologizing the strength of the Right to Life has had its purpose though; for it has helped shift the blame for the current difficulties in obtaining abortion to a few rowdy right-wingers instead of where it belongs. Make no mistake. It's not the Right to Life that's restricting access to abortion. If you really want to know who's responsible, consult your doctor. [1]

It is Cole's contention that the medical profession, through its control of hospital abortion committees that must approve all therapeutic abortions, is restricting women's access to abortion by applying an unnecessarily strict interpretation of the provisions laid down in the Criminal Code. They do so, she further argues, with the intention of exerting and maintaining control over women's reproductive capacity and our sexuality.

Cole's article was a much-needed step toward demystifying the power of the Right-to-Life, and her analysis of the medical control of all aspects of reproduction – birth control and childbearing as well as abortion – is compelling and cogent. But doctors' role in abortion access is somewhat more complex than her analysis admits. For it is not accurate to say that doctors are concerned just to *restrict* access to abortion. Relatively few doctors are totally opposed to abortion in all circumstances, just as relatively few believe that abortion should be available to women on demand. And though there is a wide spectrum of opinion within the medical profession, there are, in fact, many situations in which the majority of doctors are only too willing to advise or perform an abortion. As we have seen in Chapter Five, for example, most doctors actively counsel abortion in the case of a deformed fetus. The same is true with most cases of teenage pregnancy, and becomes more true the younger the woman is. Some doctors are more than happy to perform an abortion (and, often, sterilization as well) for a poor woman, especially if she is a native, black or another visible minority, or if she has "too many" other children who are already "a burden to the taxpayers."

On a global scale, doctors have been in the forefront of the worldwide liberalization of abortion laws that has taken place over the past three decades. In this their influence has far outweighed that of the advocates of women's right to control their own bodies. In fact, the liberalization of abortion laws in most countries preceded the rise of the "second wave" of feminism in the late sixties and early seventies. Sad to say, doctors' support for increased access to abortion was not founded on a commitment to women's choice, but on their support for population control efforts of which the abortion law reforms were only a part. Dr. Wendell Watters, a Canadian psychiatrist who was a leading figure in the abortion law reform efforts in the early seventies, is a good representative of this point of view. His 1976 book *Compulsory Parenthood* is an excellent historical overview of abortion and a penetrating analysis of the irrationalities and inequities in Canada's current abortion legislation. But Watters, while arguing passionately for the reproductive rights of women and couples, makes clear in the course of his argument that his major concern is what he calls the "world's population burden," specifically, the proliferating populations of the underdeveloped nations which are, in his view, a threat to the world economy and political stability. His main aim, in a global sense, in arguing for abortion reform is not to increase reproductive options, but to restrict the reproductive freedom of those who, in his words, "procreate blindly and indiscriminately."[2]

There has in fact been a major shift in doctors' attitudes toward both abortion and contraception in the past two or three generations. Most doctors were morally opposed to the dissemination of birth control information as late as the thirties and forties. But by the time the amendments to the Criminal Code legalizing both contraception and abortion came down in 1969, the medical profession in Canada, as well as throughout the developed nations, was firmly behind the philosophy of family planning, of which abortion services were an integral part. So to suggest that doctors always seek to restrict access to abortion is inaccurate. The problem is not whether they are in favour of abortion or not, but as Cole says, their belief that *they* should have the power to decide who shall or shall not have an abortion. And this medical control does not stop with abortion, but extends to all aspects of our reproductive capacity.

Doctors largely control access to contraception as well as the conditions under which we give birth. Although this state of affairs is now generally considered to be normal and appropriate, in fact the medical control of the means of reproduction is a relatively recent historical development, as we shall see in the next chapter. In contemporary North American society, the control by doctors of women's reproductive capacity is part of the general tendency of modern medicine to appropriate more and more aspects of living under its domain. Ivan Illich has used the phrase "the medicalization of life" to describe this phenomenon. Medical control of reproduction is also an aspect of what American sociologist Irving Kenneth Zola has described as the "social control" function of the modern health care system. It exists, he argues, not primarily to make us well but to reinforce the social status quo and to control our behaviour accordingly. Feminists, of course, have exposed the health care system as an instrument of sexism and the social control of women, and the medical control of reproduction is the bottom line of this control. Seen in this light, the threat to our freedom to choose abortion emerges as only one aspect of a much larger threat to our reproductive freedom: patriarchal society, through its "henchmen," the medical profession, has waged and continues to wage a long struggle to wrest control of reproduction from women through unsafe birth control methods, high-technology childbirth, and, much more recently, a host of genetic engineering techniques and artificial reproductive technologies that may well make women superfluous to the whole reproductive process.

Contraception

Since the 1950s there has been a veritable revolution in the field of contraceptive technology. The so-called "barrier methods," the diaphragm and the condom, which along with chemical spermicides and withdrawal were the most common and most effective means of birth control prior to the sixties, have been steadily joined by a line of newer contraceptives – the Pill, the IUD, the injectable Depo Provera – which in many ways signal a fundamental departure from the fertility control of the past. All of the newer contraceptives, unlike the older methods with the exception of the diaphragm, are under medical control, and are available to women only through contact with doctors. The newer methods are the result of sophisticated medical research, unlike most of the barrier and spermicide methods, which have their origins in folk medicine and lay technology. (An exception is the IUD, which is a descendant of old folk methods of veterinary birth control that involved inserting foreign objects into the uteri of animals to prevent conception.) The popular view of this revolution in contraceptive technology is that it has been a great boon to women, has contributed to our sexual liberation and has made reproductive freedom for women a reality for the first time in history.

This line of thought has come increasingly under attack from feminists over the past decade. For the truth is that much of this sexual "freedom" has been illusory: the real effect of the contraception revolution, as Germaine Greer and others have pointed out, has been to make us more sexually available to men, while robbing us of our freedom to say "no" to intercourse. More important, for purposes of this discussion, is the fact that much of the "progress" of these technological advances in birth control has been at the expense of our health, our fertility and sometimes our lives. The health hazards of the Pill, the IUD and Depo Provera are well known and widely documented, and warrant only a brief mention here. The Pill is associated with everything from vitamin B6 and folic acid deficiencies to a higher risk of stroke and heart disease. IUD users run a high risk of developing Pelvic Inflammatory Disease, a condition that produces massive scarring of the tissues of the reproductive tract and, often, permanent sterility. Depo Provera has been associated with breast cancer in dogs, vaginal bleeding and prolonged temporary as well as permanent sterility. In contrast, the health risks of the barrier and spermicide methods are relatively minor, and are usually confined to allergic reactions and irritations from a particular chemical or material. In 1981 a group of researchers reported a tentative link between spermicide use and subsequent birth defects in offspring, but so far their results have not been duplicated.

The technological revolution that has produced these hazardous new contraceptives is not, however, a case of a simple male plot to harm women, as a few feminists have suggested. The "plot," such as it is, is rather more complicated. For the singular feature that these and even newer methods under investigation share is what might be called their *invasive* character. In the case of the IUD, the body is literally invaded by a foreign agent. Many experts hypothesize that the reason it works (when it does — the IUD has a failure rate of 5 to 20 percent) is that the body's immunological system, in trying to expel the "invader," sets up a chronic inflammation in the lining of the uterus that prevents implantation of a fertilized egg. The Pill and other hormonal methods of birth control might be viewed as chemical invaders: their effects on the body are not local (as in the case of a vaginal spermicide, for instance), but systemic. That is, they actually alter the basic body chemistry, which is why they have such varied and wide-ranging effects. As Barbara Seaman points out in *Women and the Crisis in Sex Hormones,* the so-called "side effects" of the Pill are really a misnomer: they are as much "effects" of the drug as is the suppression of ovulation. In some ways the action of these invasive methods of birth control on the body are analogous to chemical pesticides and industrial processes that achieve a desired effect but at great cost to the balance of the ecosystem. Similarly, the result of this invasive, systemic, ultimately "unecological" approach is contraceptives that are very effective, but at great cost to health.

Just as important is the achievement of contraception that is removed from the site of sexual intercourse itself. All of the older methods involve some action around the time of intercourse, and this is the source of our longstanding dissatisfaction with them: they inhibit the spontaneity of sex. And the supposed "liberating" aspect of the newer methods lies precisely in the fact that they require no action, no choice, no volition of either partner at the time of sexual contact, and thus make for "better" sex. Some feminists, however, are sceptical of this view. The Vancouver Women's Health Collective, for instance, has argued that the joint responsibility involved in the various barrier methods can actually improve a sexual relationship by demanding increased commitment and communication on the part of both partners.

The deeper aim in developing contraception that is removed from the site of sexual intercourse is that it is also that much further removed from the action or volition of the individual woman. This is a reflection of the fact that modern birth control methods have been developed primarily to control population, *not* to achieve fertility control for individual women. From a population control standpoint, particularly in developing countries with large peasant populations where medical resources are scarce, the less individual volition involved in fertility control, the better. This is why Depo Provera, an injectable contraceptive whose effectiveness lasts for more than three months at a time, has proven so popular in Third World family planning programs, though it has never been approved for use as a contraceptive in North America. The makers of Depo Provera, Upjohn, have been lobbying the U.S. and Canadian governments intensively for years to reverse this policy. Depo Provera has been advocated by many family planning experts for women who are, in their view, too "illiterate, unreliable or irresponsible" to use other forms of birth control requiring more individual motivation or instruction. The thrust of most contraceptive research – the priorities of which women have little or no role in setting – is to reinforce this removal of control from the individual woman. A good example is the still-experimental anti-pregnancy "vaccine" based on the hormone Human Chorionic

Gonadotrophin (HCG), the development of which has been partially funded by the Canadian government. Like Depo Provera, the anti-pregnancy vaccine would be given to women by injections that would be effective for up to a year or more. Other contraceptive approaches on the horizon are even more frightening: Germaine Greer reports that some population experts are giving serious consideration to the development of contraceptives that could be introduced into the food or water supplies of Third World countries. And the major emphasis of world-wide family planning programs is still on the contraceptive "method" that eliminates individual control most effectively of all: sterilization.

Invasive contraceptive methods not only achieve population control aims, but reinforce the medical control of women's reproduction. And they have a direct impact on abortion, for without access to abortion as a backup for contraceptive failure, women are more and more forced to turn to invasive methods, because of their generally higher effectiveness rates. Even there, the myth that we need invasive methods because the "old-fashioned" ones don't work doesn't hold water: many people are unaware, for instance, that the condom, combined with contraceptive foam, is considerably more effective than the IUD, and almost as effective as the Pill. The Vancouver Women's Health Collective has argued eloquently for a sympathetic reappraisal of the tried-and-true barrier methods. And along with other women's health activists, they call for a radical redirection of priorities in contraceptive research, into avenues that will wrest control of reproduction from the multinational drug companies, the medical profession and the population control establishment, and put it back where it belongs, in the hands of women.

Childbirth

Just as women do not have the means to control our own fertility, we do not control the conditions under which we give birth. The invasive character of modern birth control methods is magnified in what is termed the "medical management" of childbirth. Modern obstetrics views birth as an essentially dangerous, pathological process requiring a high level of medical and surgical intervention in order for things to "go right." With this ideology, doctors have convinced modern women that we cannot "give birth," but that we must be managed, monitored and delivered by medical experts. The hazards of modern hospital-based childbirth are well documented and perhaps even more widely known than the hazards of modern-day birth control. Despite the considerable influence of the natural child-birth movement, drugs are still widely used to induce labour, slow down labour and manage pain. Drugs, of course, have an important place in childbirth, and few advocates of natural birth would argue that they should never be used. But drugs such as Pitocin, which stimulate labour contractions, and various sedatives and painkillers, have been shown to pose significant hazards to the fetus. Flagrant overuse of these drugs is far from unheard of on Canadian obstetrical wards. Only recently one Ontario hospital was reported to be routinely giving a sleeping medication to women who arrive in labour in the middle of the night, to avoid having to call their doctors to the hospital. As with contraception, invasive technology is more and more being introduced into the birth process. The most outstanding example of this trend is the popularity of electronic fetal monitoring (EFM), which has become standard practice in many hospitals even for low-risk, relatively uncomplicated labours. The EFM, a device used to detect fetal distress, prevents the labouring woman from moving around, keeps her in a horizontal position and in some cases appears to be itself a *cause* of fetal distress. Another example of invasive medical management of childbirth is the dramatic rise in the last ten years of the rate of Caesarian section. While a generation ago Caesarians were relatively rare, averaging no more than 10 percent of all deliveries, in some urban areas the rates are now as high as one-quarter to one-third of all births. One of the reasons for the increase is the overuse of the EFM, which can cause or inaccurately pick up fetal distress, leading in some cases to unnecessary Caesarians.

The medical control of childbirth, like the medical control of contraception, is a relatively recent historical phenomenon. Until the early part of this century (and in many places in Canada until only the last ten to twenty years) most births took place in the home, not in hospitals, and most labouring women were attended not by male doctors but by female midwives who were neighbours, friends or relatives. As writer and childbirth researcher Janis Catano makes clear, the shift in birthing practices from home to hospital and from midwives to doctors has *not* resulted in greater health and safety for mothers and infants. It has, however, accomplished the medical and professional control of childbirth, and increased the developing stranglehold of the medical profession on the total control of women's reproductive capacity. Today, fortunately, a strong birth consumer movement has arisen to reverse the trend, with a growing commitment to alternatives like home births and out-of-hospital birth centres, as well as to efforts to make hospital birthing policies more responsive to women and their babies' needs. The revival of midwifery and the movement to secure legal recognition for midwives is also a critical part of the struggle against what feminist poet Adrienne Rich has called "the theft of childbirth," and to reclaim it for women.

Genetic Engineering and Reproductive Technology

The deepest philosophical issue beneath the abortion question is the extent to which, in the name of freely chosen ends, biological realities can be manipulated, controlled and set aside. This is a very old problem, and the trend toward abortion on request reflects the most recent tendency in modern thought – namely, the attempt to subordinate biology to reason, to bring it under control, to master it. It remains to be seen whether procreation can be so easily mastered.[3]

The past decade has seen an enormous range of new technologies and techniques designed to master the biological process of reproduction, to bring it under the control of reason, as Daniel Callahan suggests above. These cover everything from amniocentesis to fetal surgery to so-called test-tube babies. While feminists have addressed the issue of reproductive control in the areas of abortion, birth control and childbirth, we have barely begun to develop a response to this new and burgeoning area, despite its even greater potential threat to our control of our reproduction. Our failure to respond is perhaps understandable, given that the area is new, evolving rapidly, and so highly technical that it is exceedingly difficult for the layperson to grasp the actual techniques, much less the issues involved. The situation is not helped by the media, which to date have taken a largely uncritical, almost cheerleader-like stance toward the phenomenon, trumpeting the birth of each new test-tube baby as they might report the winner of the Stanley Cup.

Unlike those involved with contraceptives and childbirth, the techniques and issues here are not at all widely known or understood, so some more detailed discussion is in order. What might be called the new technology of reproduction comprises two distinct areas that nevertheless overlap considerably. One of these is the area of medical genetics, and includes many techniques like amniocentesis and genetic counselling that are already widespread practices. Modern developments in medical genetics are popularly referred to by adherents and detractors alike as "genetic engineering." Put somewhat crudely, genetic engineering aims at improving the "product" of reproduction – the baby – through a variety of means: prenatal diagnosis combined with selective abortion, treatment of fetal disorders and fetal surgery *in utero,* even actual manipulation of the genetic structure. Prenatal diagnosis, of course, is already on the way to becoming routine, especially for older women, and encompasses techniques like amniocentesis, ultrasonography, and newer, more experimental measures such as chorion biopsy, which like amniocentesis involves extracting sample tissue from the fetal sac but which, unlike it, can be performed in the first trimester of pregnancy. Treatment of fetal disorders in the womb, while still for the most part experimental and limited in scope, is becoming more and more of an issue as advances are made in prenatal treatment of such conditions as hydrocephalus. And manipulation of the genetic structure, still largely experimental as far as human reproduction is concerned, is already a fact in some areas, like sex selection. As we have seen earlier in this book, sex selection through amniocentesis and selective abortion is already a reality, though not yet widespread. Of even greater concern, however, are techniques that can determine sex before conception, like sperm-splitting, which separates out the X (female) and Y (male) chromosomes in sperm. Sperm-splitting, combined with artificial insemination, can result in a fetus of the desired sex. One enterprising California doctor has already patented and marketed a sperm-splitting technique that separates out Y chromosomes, to meet the demand for what a sizable body of research on sex preferences suggests will be overwhelmingly for male children. Another form of genetic manipulation, albeit one based on dubious genetic principles, is that of banking the sperm of so-called "genius" or high-achieving males to breed babies of "superior stock" by artificial insemination. One such sperm bank, the Repository for Germinal Choice, was set up a few years ago by California entrepreneur Robert Graham to house the sperm of Nobel Prize winners and other high achievers, and has already "produced" several babies. Graham and cohorts stress that they will only inseminate suitably high-IQ women, but make clear that they think that the real "gene power" comes from the male, an assumption that flies in the face of modern genetic principle.

Nobel Prize sperm banks, though sensationalistic and clearly on the fringe of medical genetics, highlight the eugenic assumptions inherent in many genetic engineering techniques that are currently being practised and researched. Though there are many benign potential uses for these techniques, they nevertheless involve making judgements about which human traits are desirable and which are not. For the most part it is the medical community making these judgements, which are in fact moral, social and political decisions, not medical ones. Even in cases where the decision is supposedly left in the hands of parents, such as amniocentesis, we have seen that doctors are far from impartial, and exert all kinds of subtle and not-so-subtle influence over the outcome. Much of the ideological under-pinning of genetic engineering comes from a philosophy of human perfectibility that is based on the manipulation and technological control of the natural environment and life processes. An enthusiastic proponent of this view is bioethicist Joseph Fletcher, who advocates all manner of genetic engineering measures in the interest of achiev-ing "quality control" and ending what he calls "reproductive roulette." But who can say whether ridding ourselves of certain diseases and handicaps is a good thing for the human race? Who can be certain that extensive tampering with the human gene pool will not have unforeseen harmful, even horrendous, consequences for future generations? And, perhaps most importantly, who is to make these far-reaching decisions?

The other area of the new technology of reproduction has been referred to, not entirely accurately, as "artificial reproduction," and encompasses a variety of techniques that intersect with natural processes to bring about conception. Many of these techniques are well beyond the experimental stage, like *in vitro* fertilization (IVF) and some, like artificial insemination by donor (AID) have been in widespread use for many years. Artificial reproduction in some cases includes genetic engineering under its rubric, but its main aim is to achieve reproduction by what might be termed extra-natural means. Most of the techniques that fall within it have been developed to help treat infertility, but have implications far beyond that limited aim, only some of which can be discussed here.

Not all artificial reproduction involves spectacular, high-tech measures. AID is a perfectly simple, straightforward technique that can be done as easily in the home as in a doctor's office. There are increasing reports in recent years of both lesbian and heterosexual women achieving pregnancies through self-insemination with sperm from friends or anonymous donors, using turkey basters or other simple home implements. The offspring are sometimes referred to as "baster babies." Though AID has been in use for over thirty years in North America, it has been shrouded in secrecy and only now are some of the problems associated with it – legal, social and, for some, moral – being widely discussed. Some feminists have argued that AID is an important element of women's reproductive choices, and the Feminist Women's Health Centre in Oakland, California, set up a sperm bank a few years ago to make AID available to lesbians and single heterosexual women. Canadian women have also gotten into the act. A group of Windsor, Ontario, women started an artificial insemination service in 1982, to the consternation of local doctors. Said Dr. Al Yuzpe of the University of Western Ontario, "It's another women's self-help group taking medicine out of the hands of physicians."[4]

A related technique that has attracted much media attention in recent years is surrogate mothering, through which a woman agrees to be artificially inseminated by a man to whom she surrenders the child after birth. Though the child is biologically hers, she is in effect carrying it for the man and, usually, his wife. (It is important to note that this use of the term "surrogate mother," though popular, is a misnomer. The "surrogate" in this case is the real, biological mother. A true surrogate is one who agrees to carry to term an embryo transferred from another woman's body. See the discussion of embryo transfer below.) Surrogate mothering has proved to be much more controversial than AID, partly because of the implication it carries of "baby-selling," since most surrogates do it only for a fee. Feminists, to the extent that we have responded to the phenomenon, have been curiously divided on the issue. Some have argued that surrogate mothering is a legitimate option, from the point of view that women have the right to use our bodies as we wish. Others have reacted with horror to the idea of women as mere reproductive vessels, and have argued that selling our reproductive capacity because we need money does not constitute real choice, but is simply another form of exploitation. Because of the complex legalities and the highly charged emotional atmosphere surrounding it, surrogate mothering will probably remain a minor element in the artificial reproduction repertoire, and may well be made redundant by some of the newer treatments for infertility like *in vitro* fertilization and embryo transfer.

"Test-tube baby" is the popular phrase for a child conceived by *in vitro* fertilization and is, again, a misnomer, because conception takes place in a glass petri dish, not a test tube. IVF involves a complex three-stage process whereby a woman's ripe eggs are surgically removed from one of her ovaries, transferred to a petri dish where they are fertilized by her partner's sperm, then reintroduced into the uterus in the hope that at least one will implant and develop. The success rate, even with multiple embryos, is not high – about 30 percent. Usually the woman has taken a fertility drug prior to IVF to encourage her body to produce more than the single ripe egg that is usually produced in each monthly cycle. The "extra" embryos or fertilized eggs, if they are not reimplanted, are either frozen for future attempts or discarded. The ethics of destroying surplus embryos or using them for research is hotly debated, and is a perfect example of an "ethical" problem that has been created by biomedical technology. Right-to-Life groups have argued that these embryos constitute human life, and one group in Australia charged that the IVF team at a Melbourne hospital was "treating embryos with about as much respect as frozen peas." The Australian researchers countered just as passionately that the freezing technique was an effort to preserve life, and though it involved the loss of some embryos (a certain number are inevitably damaged during the thawing process) it was more preferable than simply discarding the surplus embryos after each procedure. At this writing two successful births have resulted from pregnancies achieved with the use of frozen and thawed, as opposed to fresh, embryos – one in Australia and one in the Netherlands.

The final stage of the IVF technique, embryo transfer (ET), has also been used to bring about pregnancies by removing a fertilized egg from one woman and transferring it to another. In most cases the fertilization is achieved by AID with the sperm of the "host" mother's husband, which makes it a version of surrogate motherhood in which the "baby" is delivered to the parents long before birth, rather than after. In another, related technique, donated eggs from third-party women can be used for IVF, a procedure that is the female counterpart of AID or sperm donation.

All of these techniques have been used successfully in human reproduction, though so far their use has been limited to a small number of hand-picked couples who, for the most part, have had to pay handsomely for the procedure. There are many other techniques being investigated that so far have not been used successfully on humans, but may well be in the not-too-distant future. Among them are: ectogenesis (literally "produced outside"), the maintenance and development of a fetus in an "artificial womb" environment; parthenogenesis or "virgin birth," in which reproduction is achieved from the female egg alone without fertilization by the male, a process that occurs naturally in some plant and animal species, and which has been achieved in the laboratory with mice and, at this writing, a single human egg that developed to the eight-cell stage and was subsequently destroyed by the researchers; and cloning, or asexual reproduction from a single cell of an organism that results in a genetic "carbon copy" of the original. Cloning also occurs in plants and lower animals, and has been successfully carried out in laboratory animals and even in humans, according to one popular writer, David Rorvik, whose book, *In His Image: The Cloning of a Man* is dismissed as fiction by most serious researchers.

Artificial reproduction is one of the "growth industries" of modern medicine. IVF clinics have mushroomed across Canada in the past few years; there are now six in operation, with others planned. Research centres in Britain, Australia and the U.S. have engaged in a kind of global race since the late seventies for "firsts" – first IVF baby, first IVF of a frozen embryo, first successful embryo transfer to a surrogate. One of the centres, Monash University in Melbourne, Australia, at one point adopted the tasteless practice of issuing bulletins on the number of successful IVF pregnancies: "Monash 8, rest of the world, 2." Because of its high-tech profile, artificial reproduction enormously enhances the reputations of the institutions involved in it and of obstetrician-gynecologists, who traditionally have enjoyed a fairly low status among surgical specialties, and been dismissed as mere "womb scrapers and baby catchers."

At this stage artificial reproduction techniques are confined to helping the infertile have children, and doctors working in the field justify their work with the laudable sentiment that they are "relieving the anguish of the infertile." Infertility presently affects about 15 percent of the population in North America, though this appears to be on the increase, for reasons that will be discussed below. IVF and other reproductive technologies are very expensive and at present are applicable only to a small proportion of infertility problems. Some have questioned whether the expense is justified to solve what is not, strictly speaking, a health care problem and which affects such a relatively small segment of the population. Some feminists have embraced this position, arguing that the real problem is our cultural conditioning around fertility, and that the solution lies not in medical techniques but in social responses like shared parenting. Such a response, while reasonable on its face, tends to dismiss the anguish and desperation that infertility brings. Barbara Menning, a feminist and founder of the infertility support network called RESOLVE in the U.S., has argued compellingly that techniques such as IVF must be developed and made available to the infertile as an option.

> Let those of us who are infertile decide whether we are willing to subject ourselves to the instrumentation and intervention necessary to unite ovum and sperm and reimplant the conceptus in our bodies. Let *us* make informed consent, since we will incur the risks.[5]

One way out of the impasse is to ask why so much in the way of resources and research money is being poured into "curing" infertility while comparatively little goes into prevention. Infertility is variously viewed as a state of nature, God's will or an unavoidable scourge, but it is becoming increasingly clear that infertility has concrete, discernible causes, many of which are environmental, or worse, iatrogenic, meaning caused by medical treatment. Canadian writer Nancy Miller Chenier, for example, has extensively documented a number of known workplace hazards to both the male and female reproductive systems in *Reproductive Hazards at Work*. Common industrial substances such as lead, mercury and vinyl chloride are known to reduce sperm counts and impair the fertility of male workers exposed to them. DES, a drug that was used widely in the fifties and sixties to prevent miscarriage, has been found to cause reproductive abnormalities and infertility in many of the sons of women who were given it during pregnancy. It is also associated with a high rate of infertility in the daughters of the women who took it during pregnancy. Pelvic Inflammatory Disease (PID) and other conditions that can cause infertility in women have reached near epidemic proportions in recent years. One of the reasons for this is the widespread popularity of the IUD, which greatly increases a woman's risk of developing PID. Another contraceptive, Depo Provera, also causes infertility in some of the women who use it.

Some experts have suggested that the apparent rise in both male and female infertility in recent years may be due in part to widespread exposure to a broad spectrum of environmental hazards: toxic chemicals in the food chain, nuclear fallout, chemical dumps and so on. Until a few years ago DES, for example, was used as a growth hormone to fatten cattle for the beef market in both the U.S. and Canada, and health officials report they are still encountering beef contaminated with DES because some producers have been ignoring the ban on its use.

Obviously not all infertility is preventable, iatrogenic or environmentally caused. But we might well look sceptically at reproductive technology as a solution to infertility when we realize that the people who are now bringing us IVF are the same people who brought us DES, Depo Provera and the IUD. The same mentality that has helped cause infertility in the name of the medical management of reproduction now seeks to cure it by the same unecological means. While acknowledging Barbara Menning's point that "technology owes infertile couples this option known as in vitro fertilization, since they have often been victims of other technologies" we also must ask whether reproductive technology, taken *in toto,* is really a kind of "technological fix," an illusory "solution" that is part and parcel of the ideology that created the problem in the first place, and that may in the long run only compound it. For while reproductive technologies are now being limited to "benign" uses – helping the infertile conceive – their potential for misuse is enormous. And women, particularly, have reason to wonder whether the ultimate aim of all these efforts is to relieve the anguish of the infertile or to extend male control of women's reproductive capacity to unprecedented lengths. This would mean that men would not only dictate when and how we shall or shall not reproduce but would also assume full control of the act of reproduction itself, replacing, to the extent that it proves possible, biological life processes with technological measures. Is the real aim, as many adherents claim, to "help nature along," or to control nature in the same way we have attempted to control the environment?

These questions are routinely dismissed by medical technocrats as extremist feminist ravings, but are they? We already see this kind of thinking in a milder form, in the way that the medical "team" takes credit for births that are the product of technological management. But is this just a bit of deserved self-congratulation after a job well done? Or do some men really wish to appropriate the act of reproduction to themselves? Let us look at some of the attitudes of those who are advocates of reproductive technology. Joseph Fletcher, for example, is a noted bioethicist who has written extensively on reproduction. He is an unabashed enthusiast for virtually all forms of reproductive technology in the interest of creating "fewer but better" babies. Fletcher's main concern seems to be that the irrationality and unpredictability of natural, biological reproduction militates against this stated aim, and he sees technological intervention as the only way to harness these unruly biological processes. He describes the present era of technological experimentation and intervention in reproduction as "a steady movement toward converting the *dark* and *ominous* secrets of biological life into lighted and manageable reality" (my emphasis). Elsewhere he states:

> Contrary to popular sentiment the womb is a very dangerous place – a hazardous environment. The glass womb will offer a much safer and more easily monitored container for fetuses, a place where they can be more easily manipulated for treatment and *salvation* (emphasis mine).[6]

Fletcher not only wants to "save" fetuses from the dark, ominous wombs of their mothers, he also wants to save women from ourselves. It is disturbing for a feminist to read Fletcher's use of the rhetoric of women's liberation to bolster his case for technological management of reproduction. Arguing that women are not "baby machines" and that artificial reproduction will finally create the conditions for women's complete sexual liberation, Fletcher generously offers to relieve us of the drudgery and messiness of biological birth and to "liberate" us from the burden of childbearing altogether. Fletcher also became well-known in the seventies as an advocate of "situation ethics" and of liberal access to abortion. But his views on abortion have to be seen in the overall context of his belief in the necessity to assert control over every aspect of biological reproduction. "Contraception and sterilization only control quantity," he says. "*Quality* control is achieved by a combination of the new fetal medicine with selective abortion."[7] Elsewhere he indicates that he is solidly opposed to any "sanctity of life" position and even advocates experimentation on live aborted fetuses. Fletcher is a good illustration of the fact that a liberal position on abortion is in no way synonymous with a commitment to women's right to control our bodies. He presents himself as a friend of women, but we might well say that with friends like these, who needs enemies?

Robert Francoeur, a biologist, has also written sympathetically about the new reproductive technologies in his book *Utopian Motherhood*. His enthusiasm is considerably more restrained than Fletcher's, and he at least entertains the notion that the effects of artificial reproduction may not all be beneficial. For the most part, however, he shares Fletcher's view that biological reproduction is a kind of "mistake" of nature that needs technological correction. If anything, he celebrates the separation of sex and reproduction more enthusiastically than does Fletcher, and also seeks to relieve women of the onerous burden of pregnancy and birth. To that end he looks forward to the development of the artificial womb, which he calls an "extracorporeal membrane oxygenator" or EMO. Both Francoeur and Fletcher see population control and genetic control as inseparable, and inherently desirable for the human race. For both, technological control of, and even replacement of, biological reproduction is the means to this end.

Bernard Nathanson was the self-confessed "Abortion King" of New York during the early seventies when he was director of the Centre for Reproductive and Sexual Health. Although he underwent a radical conversion of his ideas in the late seventies and went over to the anti-abortion camp, Nathanson announced in his book *Aborting America* that he had arrived at the solution to the abortion dilemma, a way to reconcile a woman's right to end an unwanted pregnancy with the fetus's right to live. Nathanson's "solution" is, of course, a technological one:

> The abortion of the future, then, will consist simply of early detection of the [fetus], removal of [it] from the unwilling mother, and transfer either to a life-support system or re-implantation into a willing and eager recipient.[8]

Here we have the familiar arsenal of transplanted embryos and artificial wombs. Elsewhere in his book Nathanson looks forward to the day when "fantastic" life-support systems will routinely sustain premature infants and aborted fetuses as small as one-eighth of a pound. He dismisses the traditional reverence for birth as mere "mythology" and the act of birth itself as an "insignificant event," thereby disposing of any illusions women might harbour about being active, aware agents in the birth process.

There is an inescapable subtext to all this desire to "manage" reproduction, and it points to a deep fear and loathing of biological life processes, of the body itself and, specifically, of women's bodies. If wombs are dark and hostile, if birth is, at best, insignificant, and at worst, a painful, messy mistake of nature, could women really wish for anything other than to be relieved of it? But is our biology really so terrifying, so disgusting? Or have we come to see it that way through a patriarchal smokescreen that fears the biological precisely because it cannot control it? The real question is: is our problem biological or ideological? And how should feminists respond to these efforts to appropriate our reproductive capacity and sever it from its biological roots?

Feminists have been committed to the idea of reproductive control as long as it resides with women themselves. This is why so much of our energy has gone into fighting for access to birth control, sterilization and abortion. But artificial reproductive technologies represent a whole other level of control. How have feminists responded to them? There is a strain of utopianism in feminist thought around reproduction that predates the actual implementation of the new technologies. This strain goes right back to the utopian communities of the nineteenth century, and views reproductive management in a generally favourable light. The most prominent modern-day advocate of this view among feminists has been Shulamith Firestone, whose *Dialectic of Sex* was one of the influential books that heralded the "second wave" of feminism in the late sixties. Firestone proposed universal artificial reproduction as the core of a program to eradicate the biological family, which she sees as the basis of women's oppression. In Firestone's view, the roots of female oppression are partly ideological, but more fundamentally biological. The fact that women give birth creates a biological tie between them and children, a kind of "nurturing imperative" that, in Firestone's view, stands inexorably in the way of women's full freedom and participation in society. The only way out of this dilemma is to sever the biological bond by adopting technological reproduction and removing the obligation to reproduce the species from women's bodies altogether. Children would then be raised in communal households, cared for by adults but with no special biological ties to any "parents."

> The blood tie of the mother to the child would eventually be severed ... so that pregnancy, now freely acknowledged as clumsy, inefficient, and painful, would be indulged in, if at all, only as a tongue-in-cheek archaism ...[9]

Firestone is not specific about the methods of artificial reproduction she favours, which is not surprising, since her real interest lies in describing the societal consequences of changing the mode of reproduction.

Looked at with hindsight, Firestone's vision has the kind of static, frozen quality characteristic of many utopian schemes. Some of her ideas on communal childrearing were popular among feminists and leftists in the sixties and seventies, but even these experiments have been considerably toned down as the pendulum swings back to more "nuclear" arrangements. By and large, feminists never really jumped on Firestone's bandwagon, but her comprehensive vision of reproductive revolution has so far not been replaced.

Poet and novelist Marge Piercy has had a much greater influence on the mainstream of feminism than has Firestone. Piercy's novels chronicling contemporary women and men struggling with new ways of living have been passed around and avidly discussed by a whole generation of women who came of age in the sixties and seventies. Her third novel, *Woman on the Edge of Time,* explores many of her familiar themes but is also a distinct departure in that it includes a science fiction treatment of a future collectivist-feminist utopia in which sex roles have been eradicated and private ownership abolished. Artificial reproduction, specifically ectogenesis or artificial womb technology, is also a fundamental part of Piercy's utopian vision. On one of her "time travels" in the novel, the main character, Connie, is shown the "brooder" by her guide, Luciente.

> He pressed a panel and a door slid aside, revealing seven human babies joggling slowly upside down, each in a sac of its own inside a larger fluid receptacle. Connie gaped, her stomach also turning slowly upside down. All in a sluggish row, babies bobbed. Mother the machine. Like fish in the aquarium at Coney Island. Their eyes were closed. One very dark female was kicking. Another, a pink male, she could see clearly from the oversize penis, was crying. Languidly they drifted in a blind school. [10]

Piercy's view of the necessity to turn to artificial reproduction to break down the biological ties between women and children is remarkably similar to Firestone's. As Luciente explains:

It was part of women's long revolution.
When we were breaking all the old hierarchies. Finally there was
that one thing we had to give up too, the only power we ever had, in
return for no more power for anyone. The original production: the
power to give birth. 'Cause as long as we were biologically enchained,
we'd never be equal. And males never would be humanized to be loving and tender. So we all became mothers. Every child has three. To
break the nuclear bonding.[11]

Piercy is more explicit than Firestone about the belief, expressed here,
that women must *give up* the power bestowed upon them by biological
childbirth in order to participate autonomously and freely in a society
where all power is shared equally. Because Piercy's treatment is sci-fi
and visionary rather than a concrete prescription for the present, and
also because she is a good novelist, her view of artificial reproduction
is more palatable and attractive than Firestone's. But while her vision
of a truly egalitarian society is still a powerful and popular one among
feminists, the ambivalence toward artificial reproduction as a means
to get there remains.

Some feminists, especially lesbians and women seeking to have
children without sexual contact with men, have had a particular
interest in the development of reproductive technologies. AID, which
is by far the simplest and least "technological" of artificial reproduction techniques, is available to fulfill this role, and increasing
numbers of women are turning to it, both privately and through more
conventional medical channels. Some women are interested in further
developments in reproductive technology because they would like to
bypass male involvement in reproduction altogether, both as sexual
partners and sperm donors. Fantasies of parthenogenesis, or reproduction of the female egg without fertilization by sperm, have had a
limited but distinct history among some feminists – especially separa-
tists, who believe in living apart from men altogether – and spiritual
feminists, who have begun to explore it on a more psychic level.
These "fantasies," however, are not really so far-fetched. As we have
seen, parthenogenesis occurs in nature and has already been achieved
to a very limited degree with a human egg in the laboratory. The most
powerful appeal of parthenogenesis for these women lies of course in
the fact that it results in only female offspring, and so has formed part

of "Amazon" fantasies of an all-female world. Feminist sci-fi writer Joanna Russ's novel *The Female Man* comes out of this tradition. In it, she draws a portrait of an all-female world called Whileaway in which everyone has two "mothers" and reproduction is accomplished by the merging of two female ova (which is not, strictly speaking, a form of parthenogenesis, which involves a single, unfertilized egg). Russ's vision is not specifically technological, and involves an almost mystical union of egg with egg.

Many contemporary feminists take the view that technology itself is neutral, neither inherently good nor bad, and that everything depends on the power relations of the situations in which it is used. These women call for a "cafeteria" approach: various options are researched and made available and women can pick and choose the methods that best suit their needs. They argue that as wide a cafeteria as possible – including all the new reproductive technologies – increases the range of choice for individual women. But does it? The basic premise of the cafeteria approach, the neutrality of technology, is the subject of much debate. Are all these reproductive technologies really neutral, or are some the product of an inherently oppressive and unecological mentality? Can we really, in Barbara Ehrenreich and Deirdre English's phrase, "seize the technology without buying the ideology"? The cafeteria approach also begs the questions of safety and experimentation. We should make no mistake about the fact that women are currently serving as the guinea pigs in a vast experiment, the full consequences of which will not be known for generations. From the birth control pill right down to the latest techniques of embryo transfer, we are seeing human experimentation on a massive and unprecedented scale. Of course, there is no way these techniques can be developed for use in humans without human involvement in the research. But we have to ask whether the benefits of the technique are really worth these risks. We have to ask whether there are alternative avenues, such as investigating the causes and prevention of infertility, that might yield the same or better results, with much less risk. We have to question whether the women and men involved in this massive experiment are able to give truly informed consent, considering the uncritical hoopla that surrounds the technology and the severe social stigma attached to infertility. Finally, we must raise questions on behalf of the children who have been born and who will be "created" as a result of reproductive technology. What will be the consequences for them? Will they be harmed in ways we cannot now foresee, as the children of "miracle drugs" like DES and Thalidomide were? Will they be harmed in more subtle ways – emotionally, genetically – that may end up being impossible to link definitively with the technology used to create them? Barbara Menning is not entirely correct in saying it is infertile men and women who bear the risks of using reproductive technologies. Perhaps even more, it will be their offspring.

In the view of some feminists, we are so far from having any degree of control over the development of the new reproductive technologies that any discussion of whether they can be used to our benefit is academic. Andrea Dworkin, for example, views reproductive technology in an apocalyptic light, as a herald of what she calls "the coming gynocide" – the culmination of patriarchy's unceasing efforts toward the complete subjugation of women. For Dworkin, reproductive technology is part of the shift from what she calls the "farming model" of female oppression, in which women are objectified as cows, earth, purely reproductive vessels, to the "brothel model," in which women's reproductive functions are completely split off from their sexuality so that they can serve as exclusive sexual playthings for men, without the consequences of pregnancy. Reproductive technology facilitates this shift, which will finally make patriarchy's stranglehold over women absolute. For Dworkin, the issue is not whether the technology is intrinsically good or bad, but the social context in which it is used. But her view of the consequences of adopting technological reproduction is so bleak that we are left with the inescapable conclusion that the use of the technology is inextricably intertwined with the hatred of women. While most feminists share her fears, few would go so far in their condemnation of male motives.

[These techniques] will give conception, gestation, and birth over to men – eventually the whole process of the creation of life will be in their hands. The new means will enable men – at last – really to have women for sex and women for reproduction, both controlled with sadistic precision by men. And there will be a new kind of holocaust, as unimaginable now as the Nazi one was before it happened: something no one believes "mankind" capable of. Using now available or soon to be available reproductive technology in conjunction with racist programs of forced sterilization, men finally will have the means to create and control the kind of women they want: the kind of women they have always wanted. To paraphrase Ernst Lubitsch's Ninotchka when she is defending Stalin's purges, there will be fewer but better women. There will be domestics, sex prostitutes, and reproductive prostitutes.[12]

The diversity of feminist responses to the phenomenon of techno-logical reproduction puts to rest the notion that "feminism" is a neat, self-contained body of ideas and principles with which all feminists agree. For the issue raises some of the knottiest and most profound questions feminism has to face, and brings to the fore the complex, ambivalent relationship women have always had with our reproduc-tive capacity, which has been the source of both our greatest power and our greatest oppression. Our response to artificial reproduction is, then, inevitably tied to the way in which we view our biology. Is it a blessing, a curse, or a bit of both? And how do we then respond to these efforts to "relieve" us of it? With enthusiasm, as did Firestone and Piercy and others whose perspectives, it has to be noted, were developed nearly a decade before many of the new technologies began to be implemented? Neutrally, as the proponents of the "cafeteria" approach would maintain? With horror, as do Dworkin and many of the rest of us, in an instinctive response to the depersonalization of the new techniques, and the obvious misogyny of many of their pro-ponents? Perhaps the concern should be not with whether a given technology is inherently benign or malevolent, but with the mental-ity of the whole approach to technological reproduction – a view of nature as a malevolent force to be conquered and controlled. There is no question that many of these technologies have some benign and beneficial uses for the human community. But we have to ask our-selves: would women, if *we* were in control of the research, have come up with techniques like cloning and IVF? Would a society in which pathological fear of our biological nature was *not* endemic so enthusiastically embrace things like embryo transfer, IVF and artificial wombs?

Perhaps our repulsion is a blind, conservative fear of technology itself, what feminist philosopher Mary O'Brien has wryly termed a "new Ludditeism." Women have often been accused of conservatism, of resistance to change and progress and of harbouring an anti-technology mentality. But historically, the introduction of new technology has never been value-free, and has always resulted in a shift in the existing power relations. It is worth remembering that the Luddites, the nineteenth-century English weavers who went around destroying the new mechanized looms, were responding primarily to the loss of autonomy and control over their labour that the new machines brought with them. The effect of the new industrialization was an all-out assault on their dignity as workers and producers, a legacy that still plagues modern industrial workers.

O'Brien's work offers feminists a valuable and much-needed context in which to respond to innovations in reproductive technology. At the heart of her work is a reaffirmation of biological reproduction, and women's experience of it. In *The Politics of Reproduction,* O'Brien argues that at the core of what she terms "malestream thought" – the entire Western philosophical and political tradition – is a profoundly dualistic view of human nature. "Man" is seen to have a lower, inferior, *biological* nature and a higher, more civilized *cultural* nature. This dualism leads to the abstract, universal notion of "man" itself, which O'Brien has elsewhere described as a kind of "metaphysical ketchup" that obscures the tangible, breathing reality of a human life and renders it tasteless. This dualism also leads to men's efforts to *transcend* the biological by projecting their own biological natures entirely onto women and consigning them to the private realm.

> Transcendence is what universal man does to biology. He gets away from it. He gets into the life of the mind, and leaves the life of the body in the care of women in the private realm. [13]

According to O'Brien, this effort to transcend our biological existence has produced in malestream thought a profound denial of both death and birth, a process that she calls upon feminists to reverse. Rather than blindly accepting the dualist, patriarchal notion that everything of importance happens in the "public realm" – the world of politics, of wage labour, of intellectual discourse – we must reclaim the value of birth and the private realm to which it has been consigned.

Feminists are increasingly aware that reproduction is the central issue for women, and that the problems of women's inferiority are not biologically but culturally determined. It is not the act of childbearing nor the task of childrearing which stamps women as inferior, but the *value* which male-dominant society has given to these necessary activities of social life.[14]

Birth is central because it is the locus of the effort to "reintegrate with nature" and with our biological existence. Thus, for O'Brien, feminism

regards the reality of childbirth as a fact and a symbol of human integration with nature, and therefore rejects the ideology of "control" of nature in favour of a politics of conservation of life and its environment.[15]

O'Brien is *not* advocating a swing back to the nineteenth-century feminist view that mothering was the central function and achievement of womanhood, though her perspective inevitably shares some aspects of what is called "nurturant feminism." What she is calling for, among other things, is a reclamation of the value of our reproductive capacity and a simultaneous embracing of our biological natures, no longer to be seen as "inferior" but equal to culture. And this embracing of the biological has enormous, far-reaching consequences, both for women and for the human race as a whole. It leads to what O'Brien calls a "politics of co-operation with Nature," which struggles against, among other things, the buildup of nuclear arsenals and the wholesale destruction of the natural environment in the name of "progress." And specifically with regard to reproduction, it leads us to reject the life-denying, anti-ecological mentality that has given rise to technological reproduction, while still recognizing that some of the specific techniques can be beneficial in certain situations, and should be researched and developed in a limited way. Which means that we, women, must be in a position to set those limits and make those choices. As with abortion, with contraception, with birth itself, it is our bodies on the line. We do not at all wish to be "relieved" of our reproductive capacity, thank you very much. What we heartily wish is at long last to control it ourselves. Biological birth is indeed messy, uncontrollable, painful. It is also a profound, intense, sometimes magnificent human experience. The "burden" of our reproduction, such as it is, must be seen as the social construct that it is, not as a biological fact.

Which leads us once again to consider the role of men in reproduction. What do we mean when we talk about women controlling reproduction? Do we mean a kind of simple replacement of female for male power, so that women exert complete control over reproduction and men become, as women have been, passive, voiceless participants, mere producers of sperm? Do we in a sense "take the sperm and run"? According to O'Brien and others, it is in fact male alienation from the process of biological reproduction that has led to men's need to claim ownership of both women's reproductive power and the product of it – children. O'Brien speaks of this process as springing from the inherent uncertainty of paternity – the fact that historically men have not been able to ascertain (and still, with modern technology, cannot fully ascertain) which man is the father of which child. In this they lack a concrete, biological connection with the propagation of the species that all women have. Thus, she says

> ... the consciousness of the father is an alienated consciousness. And the history of the species shows tremendous efforts on the part of men to resolve, to unify, that gap between their experience as an individual, and their relationship to the species. [16]

Historically, once men became aware of the causal link between intercourse and reproduction, they seized upon the idea of paternity and began to define it in terms of male rights – the right to exclusive sexual relations with a particular woman, so that they could be certain of paternity, and the right to "name" the offspring, so as to publicly proclaim the fact of their paternity. The knowledge of the male role in reproduction did not lead, interestingly enough, to increased participation by men in the actual *work* of reproduction, especially the care and raising of children. This was still left to women. The overall outcome of male alienation from reproduction has been an unceasing, ever-expanding effort to assert control over the means of reproduction in general, while minimizing their involvement with particular children and with the nitty-gritty work of bearing and caring for them.

The mantle of this long-running war has been taken up in modern times by scientific medicine, which has worked to appropriate to itself every aspect of women's reproductive power, including now, with technological reproduction, the power to conceive and carry a fetus to term.

All this leaves us with a depressingly bleak picture, and perhaps the conviction that there is nowhere to turn but to Dworkin's apocalyptic vision, which sees no way but to exclude male experience as men have excluded women's. O'Brien, while nowhere near as alarmist as Dworkin, nevertheless appears to believe that male alienation from reproduction, and the consequences of that alienation, are inherent and unresolvable. But perhaps here we have a situation where *culture,* rather than technology, can help heal the effects of a kind of "mistake of nature." For it is undeniably true, and will always be so, as O'Brien says, that "birth is experienced differently by men and women." But if we believe ourselves to be active creators of our own history, and not helpless victims of our biological destiny (though we are inevitably bound to some extent by our biological nature) we can act upon that fact, and change its consequences in the way we live. As women, we have to work together to end the "macro" male domination of reproduction. At the same time, we, women and men alike, can work to end the male alienation from reproduction on the personal level. This means substantive involvement of men in the work of reproduction – both of their own, biological children and in the more general nurturing skills that have heretofore been seen as exclusively "women's work." This embraces everything from men attending prenatal classes and being present at their children's births to active, equal involvement in childrearing, to working in fields like child care and early childhood education. Ending male alienation from reproduction also means having men take their full measure of responsibility in the work of *preventing* reproduction – in contraception, sterilization and abortion.

Reproduction, as long as it stays rooted in the biological world, will inevitably remain more the domain of women, and men have to recognize that fact as one of the ways in which both sexes are indeed bound by our biology. But women need to acknowledge that men have a place, not on the fringes of that domain, as mere sperm producers, but at the centre, as partners, as nurturers, as parents. Perhaps the inhabitants of Marge Piercy's utopia are right when they say that women, too, must be prepared to give up some of our power in the reproductive sphere in order to free both sexes. But we do not need to do so by denying our biology. And we cannot do so without simultaneously gaining more power in the social, political and economic sphere.

CHAPTER EIGHT

RECLAIMING ABORTION

OVER THE PAST decade, feminists active in health care issues have challenged the power of the medical profession in nearly all aspects of health care and reproduction. But, curiously, this challenge has not been extended to the medical control of abortion.

In a courageous and groundbreaking article, feminist health activist Connie Clement asks,

> Why haven't Canadian feminists fought the physician control of abortion? Abortion is among the simplest medical procedures performed, demanding far less range of knowledge and skill than attending births. The safety and cost-effectiveness of abortion provision by training paramedics has been proven in the Third World. Clearly it is possible to go one step beyond this and provide abortion by trained lay women in non-medical settings. [1]

The article, "The Case for Lay Abortion," stirred considerable controversy in the Toronto media when it was published in *Healthsharing,* a feminist health quarterly, in the winter of 1983. But the almost universal expressions of alarm from medical professionals and pro-choice activists only served to illustrate how strong is our medical conditioning, and how short our collective memory. For the medical control of abortion and other aspects of reproduction, as we have seen in the previous chapter, is in fact a relatively recent phenomenon. Prior to the twentieth century, contraception and abortion, like childbirth, were largely the province of local lay practitioners who used a variety of folk methods, some of which were effective, many of which were not. As medical techniques of abortion were greatly improved in the nineteenth century, a few doctors began providing abortions illegally, though the profession as a whole deplored the practice. The control of contraceptive information and technology was literally handed over to the medical profession in North America by Margaret Sanger in the 1920s. Sanger's move was originally strategic. She decided that the way to legalization and public acceptance of birth control was to end its "outlaw" status and to attach to it the prestige and scientific aura of medicine. This was despite the fact that the medical profession in North America had fought the birth control movement tooth and nail since its inception, and that Sanger herself, along with many other radical lay people, had become the chief providers of accurate birth control information to a public in desperate need of it.

Although contraception thus passed into medical hands from the early thirties onwards, abortion, with some exceptions, remained outside the medical sphere and continued to be provided by non-medical, so-called "quack" abortionists and a few medical mavericks. By the sixties, however, many middle- and upper-class women were able to obtain abortions from their physicians, while poor women continued to turn to illegal lay abortionists. In 1969 abortion was finally legalized in Canada under certain rather stringent conditions. Then in 1973, the momentous U.S. Supreme Court decision Roe vs. Wade effectively removed all legal restrictions on abortion in that country during the first three months of pregnancy. As a result of these developments, non-medical abortionists were put almost completely out of business in North America, and control of abortion passed into physicians' hands, thus completing the medical takeover of all aspects of women's reproduction – birth, contraception and now abortion. And just as with childbirth and contraception, it is almost universally assumed that the passing of abortion into the medical domain has been unequivocally positive, rescuing women from the hands of backstreet butchers and delivering them into the care of competent medical personnel in clean, sterile clinics or hospitals.

While no one can quarrel with the fact that the *legalization* of abortion has been a good thing for women, it is questionable whether or not the *medicalization* that accompanied legalization has been similarly to women's benefit. To explore this question we need to examine some historical developments, specifically the notion that medical abortion is always safe, while non-medical abortion is always dangerous. Interestingly, this is very close to the ideology that has arisen around medicalized childbirth. When physicians took control of birth away from midwives in the nineteenth century and moved it from the home into the hospital, physician-attended hospital birth came to be defined as "safe" while home birth with a midwife came to be defined as dangerous. This was despite the fact that childbirth had been carried out in the home with relative safety for centuries, and that the move to doctors and hospitals did virtually nothing to improve maternal and infant mortality. The shift from home to hospital and from midwife to doctor was not really the boon to women that it was presented as by the medical profession. What really occurred was an ideological shift, so that the risks associated with hospital birth came to be seen as "socially acceptable," in the words of Janis Catano, while the risks associated with the home were considered unacceptable.

Is it possible that the supposed "danger" of non-medical abortions, like non-medical childbirth, could be more ideological than real? Traditionally, abortion, like birth control, was managed by midwives and lay healers, almost always women, who were an integral part of the community and who passed their knowledge down from generation to generation. Long before the medical technology for abortion was perfected, these "wise women" had developed and refined a repertoire of folk methods of birth control and abortion. For the most part they made no distinction between the two – the sharp separation of abortion from contraception is largely a modern preoccupation. Many of these folk methods of abortion were based on herbs. Some involved inserting an object into the uterus, or other physical means like heavy lifting or massage of the abdomen. Many relied heavily on an element of magic as well as the physical action of the potion or instrument. According to social historian Linda Gordon, it is a myth that the traditional forms of birth control and abortion were always ineffective. Even the magical element should not be discounted, she says, since it may well have been effective in creating a mental state that helped prevent conception or induce abortion. Though many folk methods of abortion were both painful and dangerous, many were neither, she says. And for the most part women in past times did not have much choice in the matter.

> Women have traditionally accepted the pain and danger of abortion as matter-of-factly as they accepted the pain and danger of childbirth at other times, with the assumption that both were necessary for their own and their communities' health and welfare. [2]

Another historian, Angus McLaren, found that many of the traditional herbal abortifacients used in nineteenth-century Canada were often effective. These remedies were very widely used, he says, and played a major role in lowering the birth rate in the late nineteenth and early twentieth centuries.

The nature of lay abortion underwent a change as many of the medical techniques for inducing abortion "went underground" and were taken up by the outlaw practitioners. Many of the traditional herbal techniques began to fall into disuse in the early twentieth century. And more and more men came to be found among the ranks of lay abortionists, many of them medical doctors who were in it for the money, were alcoholics or had lost their licence to practise. (A small number of the doctors performing illegal abortions, like Dr. Henry Morgentaler, did so out of a real concern for women's safety and a political conviction that abortion was a woman's right.) It is now commonly assumed that virtually all of the illegal practitioners were dangerous quacks and butchers working in filthy quarters, and that many, if not most, women were either seriously harmed or killed by the procedure. Although there is much truth in this popular portrayal, there is considerable evidence that the danger of illegal abortion in modern times has been grossly exaggerated. In fact, according to Linda Gordon:

> There is probably more misunderstanding about abortion safety today than earlier in history, because the campaign for legalized abortion has naturally tended to exaggerate the mortality rate from illegal abortion. In fact, illegal abortions in this country have an impressive safety record. [3]

Lucinda Cisler, a feminist and one of the chief architects of the campaign to legalize abortion in the U.S., echoes Gordon's contention and takes the abortion reform movement to task for inflating the death rate from illegal abortions. Writing in the feminist anthology *Sisterhood is Powerful,* Cisler claims that, contrary to the figure of 10,000 deaths per year that had been "bandied about" by the advocates of reform, the actual numbers of deaths in the U.S. from septic abortions was closer to five hundred to one thousand per year.[4]

Compelling testimony to the fact that non-medical abortion can be done safely comes from American sociologist Pauline Bart's account of "Jane," an illegal feminist abortion collective that operated in Chicago from 1969 to 1973. Jane was started by a number of activists in the Chicago Women's Liberation Union and grew out of an abortion referral and counselling service on the University of Chicago campus. Initially involved simply in steering women to safe and relatively cheap illegal abortionists, the women in Jane gradually learned how to perform abortions themselves, and actually provided more than 11,000 abortions in their own homes in their four years of operation. During this time, the safety record of Jane compared favourably with legal abortion clinics in New York and California, and the single death that occurred was of a woman who arrived at Jane already severely infected, probably as the result of an incomplete self-induced abortion. Though the collective terminated Jane following the 1973 Supreme Court ruling, their story raises some intriguing questions about the way abortion, and indeed many medical services, are provided. For these were laywomen, with virtually no formal medical training. Yet they learned to give shots, take blood pressure, give pap smears, perform D and Cs and operate the vacuum aspirator used in first trimester abortions. They combined all this with intensive, caring counselling, and stressed to Bart their belief that the "medical" and "counselling" components of the service should not be separated. Their experience in Jane was a profound challenge to the mystique of medical expertise and professional power. As one Jane member told Bart,

> If it's necessary you can take the tools of the world in your own hands,
> and all that crap about how you have to be expert to do anything,

whether fixing your car or your vacuum cleaner or administering medical aid is just a ruse to make you feel incompetent in your own life. One thing we learned is that if you want to learn how to do something you can do it.[5]

Jane, of course, grew out of a situation of dire necessity, and the women who ran it decided that they *had* to take the tools of abortion into their own hands, because women were being harmed by other dangerous, irresponsible abortionists. But though the political context has changed, the experience of Jane is very relevant to the present abortion predicament.

It should be clear from all this that a distinction needs to be made between the perceived dangers of *illegal* abortion and the perceived dangers of *lay* or non-medical abortion. There is ample evidence that, even under illegal conditions, non-medical abortion can be done safely. Obviously, then, legalized lay abortion, if supported by medical back-up, can be provided even more safely. This is increasingly being done in many parts of the world where doctors are scarce. There are many relatively simple medical procedures that can be provided just as competently (and far more cheaply) by lesser-trained personnel when doctors are unavailable or unwilling to perform them. In the Canadian north, for example, nurse-midwives can legally assist at births, but they are not, of course, allowed to do so in more populous areas, where they would be competing with doctors. Similarly with abortion, in many parts of the Third World, midwives and other traditional practitioners are being trained to perform very early abortions, safely and at a fraction of the cost of medical abortions. Clearly, then, the case against lay abortion is based on political, not medical, concerns. Lay abortion, *if* fully supported by the state and backed up by medical services, can be offered to women with safety and caring.

But why talk about lay abortion at all? Hasn't medical abortion served our needs perfectly well? There is no question that doctors have provided us with safe, competent abortions. In a good number of cases, moreover, they do so in a caring, supportive atmosphere, and with very high medical standards. But there are many aspects to abortion and women's needs that are not and cannot be met in a medical setting. Some parallels with midwifery and the home birth movement might be instructive here. It is no accident that examples from childbirth and midwifery keep coming up in this chapter. And it is interesting to note that both the home birth and the abortion rights movements have gravitated to the notion of *choice,* because both are, in a sense, fighting for the same thing: the right to determine the conditions under which women reproduce. Non-medical childbirth and non-medical abortion are both illegal in this country. Advocates of legalized midwifery and home birth are fighting for the right to choose where, how and with whom women will give birth, and to end their "outlaw" status if they choose to go outside of the prescribed medical setting. They do so for a number of reasons. They recognize, first and foremost, that the birthing woman must be in control of her own labour and delivery, and that this control is nearly always denied her in a medical setting. They argue that the *place* of birth is absolutely integral to the progress and outcome of the birth and the woman's experience of it. Birth, they say, is not primarily a medical process, but a social, emotional and spiritual one, which medical childbirth in no way acknowledges or accommodates. Birth, they conclude, must be in the right hands, if its full human dimension is to be honoured and preserved.

This discussion of childbirth and midwifery offers us more than a parallel to abortion. It points us back to the common roots of both. As we have seen, in many traditional societies, and in much of Canada prior to the twentieth century, it was midwives, lay healers, ordinary women in the community who both assisted at births and helped women prevent or abort their pregnancies. These women involved themselves in all aspects of reproduction, and did not make the distinctions between birth, contraception and abortion that we make today. In fact, in ancient Rome the women who performed abortions were called *sagae,* which is thought to be the root word for the French term for midwife, *sage-femme.* Contemporary lay midwives resist this connection, however. Because of their overwhelming orientation toward childbearing and the joy of giving birth, and because of their profoundly spiritual approach, many midwives are uncomfortable with abortion. They have not been noticeably active in the pro-choice movement, and some, indeed, are openly opposed to abortion. Connie Clement quotes one midwife as saying, "The movements ... are not alike. One is about life and one is about death." But Vicki Van

Wagner, a Toronto midwife who is also strongly pro-choice, points out that the strict dichotomy between birth as "life" and positive and abortion as "death" and negative does not really correspond to women's experience of either:

> There is an incredible range of emotion that can be involved in most reproductive experiences. Through pregnancy, labour, birth, miscarriage and abortion, women feel pain, pleasure, joy, sorrow, fear, courage, anger and love, often simultaneously.[6]

Not a few women, for instance, become preoccupied with death during pregnancy, or experience profound depression, even suicidal feelings, after giving birth. We do ourselves no favour by feeding into the mythology that childbirth and childrearing are always joyful and fulfilling. And, as we saw in Chapter Two, abortion, though a painful and difficult decision for women, very often has strongly positive elements as well. In her article, Clement describes coming to the realization that abortion, if carried out in the right circumstances, can be a "positive and energizing event, a sometimes joyful celebration." Perhaps it is most accurate to say that *both* childbirth and abortion are approached with profound ambivalence by women, and call up a wide range of emotions that vary greatly with individuals and that need to be acknowledged and affirmed.

Whether or not midwives become involved in the provision of modern-day abortion, as they did in past times, we do need practitioners of abortion who share their best qualities and concerns. For abortion, like birth, has profound social, emotional and spiritual dimensions. Abortion, like birth, must be kept in the right hands, and, like birth, must be carried out by those who love and respect women, who believe in their right to control their own bodies and who share a deep reverence for both life and death. We need to reclaim abortion for ourselves, and free it from medical domination. This is not to say that we want no medical *involvement* in abortion. Clearly, as with childbirth, there is an important role for doctors to play in providing abortion – as backup, as consultants, to perform second trimester or more complicated abortions. What we are talking about is ending medical *control,* not only of abortion but of every aspect of women's reproduction. History has shown us how difficult this task is going to be, however, because of modern medicine's tendency to assume control of every aspect of life it touches.

We also have to reclaim abortion from so-called allies like Joseph Fletcher and biologist Garrett Hardin, who are major apologists for abortion as an element of population control. Hardin, author of an oft-cited polemic for liberalized abortion, *Mandatory Motherhood,* is also the best-known exponent of the "lifeboat theory," which views overpopulation, not inequitable distribution of global resources, as the root cause of world poverty. Hardin advocates eliminating what he calls the world's "surplus population" through compulsory family planning programs. Such programs are being carried out throughout the Third World, with varying degrees of coercion (or what family planning bureaucrats prefer to call "incentives") by organizations like the International Planned Parenthood Federation (IPPF), the Population Council, the U.S. Agency for International Development (USAID) and our own Canadian International Development Agency (CIDA). Population control is strongly supported by most governments of the developed world, and abortion is an absolutely integral part of international family planning programs. This link has been an important element in the world-wide liberalization of abortion laws, and has provided an important base of "establishment" support that many in the pro-choice movement have been reluctant to question or disturb. Because of this we have not fully explored and acknowledged the many profound differences most feminists have with these organizations, differences that centre on women's right to reproductive control, the right of Third World peoples to self-determination and their rightful share of world resources, and the inherent value and desirability of children, who are seen primarily as a "drain on resources" by population control apologists. While we may continue to work with population control advocates on specific abortion campaigns, we have to do so from a context of reproductive rights, rather than simply abortion rights. We have to make clear that our right to control our reproduction shares nothing with a population control ideology that legitimizes the control and exploitation of women's reproductive capacity in the interest of perpetuating an inequitable political and economic order.

If we were to be able to truly reclaim abortion for ourselves, what would it look like? How would it change? Here the present call for the establishment of freestanding (out-of-hospital) abortion clinics in Canada becomes pertinent. Under the Canadian Criminal Code, all abortions must be carried out in accredited hospitals, which ensures the continuing medical control of abortion. This is not the case in the U.S., where many out-of-hospital abortion clinics are operated by feminist health collectives on a non-profit basis, but many others are run by doctors and private companies. The feminist-run centres, as we might expect, have a significantly different approach and are more likely to be attuned and responsive to the whole range of needs and issues women must grapple with around abortion. By 1977 the pioneering Feminist Women's Health Centre in Los Angeles was looking at ways of dealing with the ambivalence they were encountering in women seeking abortions. One of the Centre's founders, Carol Downer, began to talk publicly about some of the thornier aspects of the abortion issue. But many of the feminist clinics do not significantly depart from the standard medical approach. They provide competent service in a generally supportive setting, but they are still a long way from true woman-controlled abortion. Similarly in Canada, the movement for freestanding clinics has so far not questioned the medical approach, but this is because, as we have seen, feminists and the pro-choice movement have not questioned it either. This whole book is an argument for an expansion and deepening of the feminist view of abortion, and a willingness to tread into areas that so far we have shunned, ignored or feared. If we are going to accept these new aspects of abortion, we have to find ways to put them into practice, to ensure that the way abortion is provided in our society reflects all of its many facets.

One of the most common objections to abortion clinics is the fear that they encourage abortion by making it "too easy." This goes with an unstated assumption that making abortion hard to get, or a negative experience, as it so often is in our hospitals, will somehow discourage women from getting one. This is simply untrue. If nothing else, the history of abortion shows beyond doubt that women *will* obtain them, legally or illegally, whether they are cheap or costly, painful or not, difficult or easy to get. Virtually no sanctions, legal or religious, have ever deterred women from getting abortions, though they have made the experience infinitely more traumatic and dangerous. The only thing that has ever significantly affected women's ability to abort has been the efficacy and safety of the methods available in any given culture at any given time. Of course clinics will make abortion "easier" for women, in that they will be able to obtain it in an atmosphere of love and support, and will not have to justify their decision and prove that it fulfills the requirements of the Criminal Code. But in terms of the personal issues, woman-run clinics may not necessarily be easier. Indeed, some women may find it harder in the short run to explore some of the more difficult and painful aspects of the abortion decision. For clinics could give women an opportunity to really explore and work through these personal issues, an opportunity that does not exist now in most hospital settings. Right now women having abortions have to summon all their inner resources just to deal with the lack of caring and even emotional brutality that sometimes greets them on hospital wards. In many cases the staff assisting at abortions don't really want to be doing them, or experience grave conflicts about terminating life when all their training stresses the preservation of life. Often there is an attitude of blame attached to abortion-seeking women that springs from a number of sources: their sexual activity, their "irresponsibility" about birth control and their rejection of their childbearing and nurturing role. There are particular stresses attached to providing abortions that have to be acknowledged and dealt with, and hospitals, in their present form, simply cannot provide this. Again the comparison with childbirth is apt: advocates of home and out-of-hospital birth have put forth similar arguments about the inability of the hospital to respond to the real needs of childbearing women. There is a whole range of emotional issues that surround all of women's reproductive experience, as we have seen. Somehow the settings we create must reflect and address this. If anything, the way medical abortions are now provided simply helps perpetuate the cycle of unwanted pregnancy, by focussing on the procedure and ignoring the woman herself and her personal context. As we saw in Chapter Two, a number of researchers have suggested that *failure* to work through the emotional issues surrounding unwanted pregnancy, rather than promiscuity or irresponsibility, is a major cause of repeat abortions.

Even the term "clinic" maintains the medical connection. We might want to think beyond it to "reproductive health centres" where midwives or other specially trained, highly committed women would help other women in every aspect of their reproductive capacity: childbearing, contraception, sterilization and abortion. These practitioners would inherit the legacy of the midwives and wise women of old, who shared their knowledge freely out of love and sisterhood, and whose contribution to women's health was distorted and denigrated in the medical takeover of women's reproduction. These modern midwives could combine the best of both worlds in a way that their foremothers could not, using their specialized training and intuitive skills backed up by the appropriate use of medical technology, in much the same way they do now for birthing women.

Our fantasies must go beyond the walls of a particular location, however, since the thrust of much recent fertility research is the development of do-it-yourself "home abortion." Two possibilities exist in this realm right now: menstrual extraction and prostaglandin suppositories. Menstrual extraction involves the insertion of a thin plastic tube through the cervix and the application of gentle suction to draw out the lining of the uterus. It is basically a simpler version of vacuum aspiration, which is the most prevalent method of first trimester abortion in North America. Unlike vacuum aspiration, it need not be carried out in a medical setting and requires only very simple implements. The great advantage of menstrual extraction, and the thing that led feminist health groups to champion it for a time, is the fact that it can be carried out in the home or clinic setting within days of a missed period, well before pregnancy can be confirmed by existing tests. Some of the U.S. feminist health centres offered menstrual extraction during the seventies, and small groups of women got together and performed it on each other. But concerns began to emerge about the efficacy of the procedure. There was evidence that it often resulted in incomplete abortion. Menstrual extraction appears to have been largely abandoned by the women's health movement, at least for the time being, though it is still being researched and used in the Third World. Its potential as a form of very early, safe abortion remains largely untapped in North America.

Prostaglandin suppositories have the potential to open up a whole new chapter in the history of abortion. Unlike menstrual extraction, in which the pregnant woman requires the assistance of at least one other person, prostaglandin suppositories allow women to abort themselves completely on their own in the privacy of their own home. Prostaglandins are substances that occur naturally in the human body and that stimulate the contraction of smooth muscle tissue. They are already widely used to induce second trimester abortions in hospitals, and a wealth of new research indicates that they can also serve as very effective abortifacients in the earliest days or weeks of a pregnancy. Like menstrual extraction, prostaglandin suppositories can be applied even before a pregnancy is confirmed. There are serious concerns about prostaglandins from the point of view of safety, however. They cause strong uterine contractions that can be extremely painful, and that can cause the uterus itself to rupture. They have a variety of other side-effects such as headache and diarrhea and can adversely affect a woman's heart and blood pressure. A good deal more research and refinement need to be carried out before these problems are resolved.

The prospect of widely available prostaglandin suppositories is both exhilarating and terrifying. They hold the potential to be what women have been seeking for centuries: an easy, safe, non-traumatic and effective way of terminating an unwanted pregnancy. They eliminate the need to undergo a surgical procedure or even to go to a hospital or clinic. They can be administered as soon as a pregnancy is suspected, or even postcoitally. They also offer the possibility of circumventing restrictive abortion laws, since in the view of some experts they are more appropriately viewed as forms of contraception known as "interceptors" like the morning-after pill. But the ramifications of "do-it-yourself" abortion are largely unknown. Do we run the risk of privatizing the abortion experience in a negative way, driving it back to the "bad old days" when women endured self-induced abortions in silent shame? And though the suppositories will likely be available only on prescription, they will be administered without any supervision. How do we know that women will use them safely? How will users know when things are proceeding normally and when to seek medical help? And what about emotional support? By *not* making it necessary for women to seek help in obtaining abortions, will we be in effect forcing them back on their own resources, which may be far from adequate, at a time when support and validation from other women is so critical?

We keep returning to the uncomfortable fact stressed by Germaine Greer that the new self-abortion methods, like the invasive contraceptive methods, are being developed primarily for population control purposes, not to increase women's choices. They offer the prospect of cheap, effective abortions for peasant populations in underdeveloped countries, and we must not delude ourselves that they will automatically be to women's benefit, either to us or to our sisters in the Third World. As we should have with the birth control pill and the IUD, let us look this gift horse in the mouth carefully before we accept it. If women are to reclaim abortion for ourselves, we will have to fight hard to exert control over how these new methods are researched and used.

There are other possibilities to explore as well. Herbs such as pennyroyal have been known to be effective abortifacients for centuries, though no one is sure why. Herbal abortifacients, like herbal remedies in general, have for the most part not been treated seriously by the medical research community. In recent years a few fertility researchers have begun to explore the tremendous range of herbal contraceptives and abortifacients. What they are discovering is that many of them, used correctly according to folkloric tradition, *do* work. Another possibility, perhaps least drastic and most ecological of all, is that of psychic abortion. Anthropologist George Devereux found considerable documented evidence of psychogenic abortion in his vast survey of abortion practices in primitive societies. And contemporary women involved in spiritual healing are quietly beginning to explore the possibility of psychic abortion in small support groups. Jeanine Parvati's book, *Hygieia: A Woman's Herbal,* contains a number of accounts of California women who claim to have induced abortion through meditation alone, or a combination of meditation and herbs. In these accounts the abortion involves far more than the use of the conscious will, and is usually accomplished with the active consent of the fetal spirit, who responds to the woman's request to leave her body. Psychic abortion is a remote, to some even absurd, proposition in our would-be rational, medicalized society. But it is not unlike the process of self-healing called creative visualization that is becoming very popular among cancer patients, and that is actively fostered by some of the pillars of mainstream medicine. If cancer patients can learn to mobilize their inner resources to contain the spread of their disease and even cure themselves, who is to say that some women could not develop similar inner powers to achieve self-abortion?

It is difficult to predict where current developments in abortion techniques will lead us. What is certain is that women's need for abortion will continue for the foreseeable future, and we have a long, difficult task ahead of us to ensure that it is provided in a way that meets all of our needs, as well as those of our partners and our children. For abortion is still a long way from being in our own hands, and the consequences of this fact impinge on every aspect of our lives. The medical control of abortion, contraception and birth has resulted in the splitting off of our reproductive capacity from our total being as women and human beings, a split that has been necessary to the continuance of sexism and patriarchal power. We must begin to heal that schism. Reclaiming our reproduction means embracing it, celebrating it as the joyous miracle that it is, while at the same time affirming that it is not the totality of our existence, that we have needs, visions and potentials as broad and varied as the rest of humanity.

NOTES

CHAPTER ONE

[1] Larry D. Collins, "The Politics of Abortion: Trends in Canadian Fertility Policy," *Atlantis,* Spring 1982, p. 3.

[2] Kathleen McDonnell, "Claim No Easy Victories: The Fight for Reproductive Rights," in Maureen FitzGerald, Connie Guberman and Margie Wolfe, eds., *Still Ain't Satisfied: Canadian Feminism Today* (Toronto: Women's Press, 1982), p. 33.

[3] Women's Liberation Movement "Brief to the House of Commons Health and Welfare Committee on Abortion Law Reform," in Janice Acton, et al., eds., *Women Unite!* (Toronto: Women's Press, 1972), p. 114.

[4] Lucinda Cisler, "Unfinished Business: Birth Control and Women's Liberation," in Robin Morgan, ed., *Sisterhood is Powerful* (New York: Random House, 1970), p. 246.

CHAPTER TWO

[1] Eileen Fairweather, "Abortion: The Feelings Behind the Slogans," *Spare Rib* 87, p. 28.

[2] Adrienne Rich, *Of Woman Born: Motherhood as Experience and Institution* (New York: Bantam Books, 1976), p. 273.

[3] Linda Bird Francke, *The Ambivalence of Abortion* (New York: Random House, 1978), pp. 99, 200.

[4] Carol Gilligan, *In a Different Voice: Psychological Theory and Women's Development* (Cambridge, Mass.: Harvard University Press, 1982), p. 111.

[5] Mary K. Zimmerman, "Psychosocial and Emotional Consequences of Elective Abortion: A Literature Review," in Paul Sachdev, ed., *Abortion: Readings and Research* (Toronto: Butterworths, 1981), p. 65.

[6] Christie McLaren, "Women suffer few serious woes after abortion, researchers say," *Globe and Mail*, May 23, 1984, p. M1.

[7] "The Right to Grieve: Two Women Talk About Their Abortions," *Healthsharing*, Winter 1983, p. 21.

[8] Ibid.

[9] Ibid., p. 20.

[10] "Protesters denounce abortion," *Toronto Star*, August 8, 1983, p. A6.

[11] Susan Borg and Judith Lasker, *When Pregnancy Fails* (Boston: Beacon Press, 1981), p. 50.

[12] "The Right to Grieve," p. 21.

[13] Zimmerman, p. 69.

[14] Gilligan, p. 80.

[15] Ibid., pp. 94-95.

[16] "The Right to Grieve," p. 20.

[17] Ibid.

[18] Gilligan, p. 76.

[19] "The Right to Grieve," p. 26.

[20] Esther R. Greenglass, *After Abortion* (Toronto: Longman Canada, 1976), p. 92.

[21] Ibid., pp. 81-82.

[22] Gilligan, p. 121.

CHAPTER THREE

[1] Linda Gordon, *Woman's Body, Woman's Right: A Social History of Birth Control in America* (New York: Grossman, 1976), p. 35.

[2] Simone de Beauvoir, *The Second Sex* (New York: Alfred A. Knopf, 1952), p. 119.

[3] Bernard Nathanson, with Richard N. Ostling, *Aborting America* (Garden City, N.J.: Doubleday, 1979), p. 213.

[4] Henry Morgentaler, *Abortion and Contraception* (Toronto: General Publishing, 1982), p. 147.

[5] Katherine Govier, "The Morgentaler Manifesto," in *Quest*, October 1983, p. 24.

[6] Michele Landsberg, "Women's group behind plan for abortion clinic," *Toronto Star*, November 4, 1982, p. B1.

[7] Lindsy Van Gelder, "Cracking the Women's Movement Protection Game," in *Ms*, December 1978, pp. 66-67.

[8] Carol Gilligan, *In A Different Voice: Psychological Theory and Women's Development* (Cambridge, Mass.: Harvard University Press, 1982), p. 21.

[9] Ibid., p. 104.

[10] Deirdre English, "The War Against Choice: Inside the Antiabortion Movement," in *Mother Jones*, February/March 1981, p. 19.

[11] Tom Harpur, "Abortion not always wrong, says pastor," *Toronto Star*, June 4, 1983, p. A13.

[12] Nathanson, p. 248.

[13] Daniel Callahan, "Abortion: Some Ethical Issues," in Thomas A. Shannon, ed., *Bioethics*, rev. ed. (Ramsey, N.J.: The Paulist Press, 1981), pp. 17-18.

[14] Gilligan, p. 58.

CHAPTER FOUR

[1] Mary K. Zimmerman, *Passage Through Abortion: The Personal and Social Reality of Woman's Experience* (New York: Praeger, 1977). See also Esther R. Greenglass, *After Abortion* (Toronto: Longman Canada, 1976).

[2] Carol Gilligan, *In a Different Voice: Psychological Theory and Women's Development* (Cambridge, Mass.: Harvard University Press, 1982), p. 89.

[3] Ibid., p. 123.

[4] Sharon Rutenberg, "What Men and Women Want from Children," *Toronto Star*, January 2, 1984, p. A14.

[5] Simone de Beauvoir, *The Second Sex* (New York: Alfred A. Knopf, 1952), p. 491.

[6] Lynn Moore, "Fathers should have right to veto abortions, group says," *Toronto Star*, June 18, 1984, p. A12.

[7] Christie McLaren, "Husband's final bid to prevent abortion is dismissed by judge," *Globe and Mail*, March 24, 1984, p. 2.

[8] "The Right to Grieve: Two Women Talk About Their Abortions," *Healthsharing*, Winter 1983, p. 20.

[9] Ibid.

[10] Linda Bird Francke, *The Ambivalence of Abortion* (New York: Random House, 1978), p. 133.

[11] Roger Wade, *For Men, About Abortion*, 1978. (Available from Roger C. Wade, P.O. Box 4748, Boulder, Colorado, 80306.)

CHAPTER FIVE

[1] *"I Support You But I Can't Sign My Name": Pro-Choice Catholics Testify*, Catholics for a Free Choice, Washington, D.C. 1982, p. 15.

2 Linda Bird Francke, *The Ambivalence of Abortion* (New York: Random House, 1978), p. 88.

3 R.F. Badgley, D.F. Caron and M.G. Powel, *Report of the Committee on the Operation of the Abortion Law* (Ottawa: Supply and Services Canada, 1977), p. 362.

4 Esther R. Greenglass, *After Abortion* (Toronto: Longman Canada, 1976), p. 77. See also Dorothy Lipovenko, "Money woes cited by abortion seekers," *Globe and Mail,* December 7, 1983, p. 5.

5 Germaine Greer, *Sex and Destiny: The Politics of Human Fertility* (London: Secker and Warburg, 1984), p. 30.

6 Jessie Bernard, *The Future of Motherhood* (New York: Penguin, 1974), p. 9.

7 Vicki Van Wagner, Letter in *Healthsharing,* Spring 1984, p. 26.

8 Lillian Newbery, "Support group helps people cope with problems of Turner's Syndrome," *Toronto Star,* April 17, 1984, p. C2.

9 Gwyneth Ferguson Matthews, *Voices from the Shadows: Women with Disabilities Speak Out* (Toronto: Women's Press, 1983), p. 101.

10 Rayna Rapp, "The Ethics of Choice," *Ms,* April 1984, p. 98.

11 Ibid., p. 100.

12 Deirdre English, "The War Against Choice: Inside the Antiabortion Movement," *Mother Jones,* February/March 1981, p. 32.

CHAPTER SIX

1 Letter, *Toronto Star,* November 5, 1983, p. B3.

2 Val Ross, "The pro-life boycott," *Maclean's,* January 30, 1984, p. 42.

3 Deirdre English, "The War Against Choice: Inside the Antiabortion Movement," *Mother Jones,* February/March 1981, p. 28.

4 Interview, "Radio Noon," CBLT Toronto, February 7, 1984.

5 Barbara Ehrenreich, *The Hearts of Men* (New York: Doubleday, 1983), p. 47.

6 Andrea Dworkin, *Right-Wing Women* (New York: G.P. Putnam's and Sons, 1983), p. 103.

7 Andrew H. Merton, *Enemies of Choice* (Boston: Beacon Press, 1981), p. 122.

8 John Brehl, "The People Who Oppose Abortions," *Toronto Star,* August 22, 1983, p. D1.

9 Paul Webster, "De Beauvoir reveals Sartre's macho ways sparked her crusade," *Globe and Mail,* May 19, 1984, p. E12.

10 Anne Finger, "Leftists should defend 'Baby Doe's' right to live, " *Guardian,* December 21, 1983, p. 19.

[11] Daniel Callahan, "Abortion: Some Ethical Issues," in Thomas A. Shannon, ed., *Bioethics,* rev. ed. (Ramsey, N.J.: The Paulist Press, 1981), p. 23.

CHAPTER SEVEN

[1] Susan G. Cole, "The Real Abortion Issue," *This Magazine,* June 1983, p. 5.

[2] Wendell W. Watters, M.D., *Compulsory Parenthood: The Truth About Abortion* (Toronto: McClelland and Stewart, 1976), p. xvii.

[3] Daniel Callahan, "Abortion: Some Ethical Issues," in Thomas A. Shannon, ed., *Bioethics*, rev. ed. (Ramsey, N.J.: The Paulist Press, 1981), p. 23.

[4] "Women start artificial insemination service," *Toronto Star,* June 26, 1982, p. 1.

[5] Barbara Menning, "In Defense of In Vitro Fertilization," in Helen B. Holmes, Betty B. Hoskins and Michael Cross, eds., *The Custom-Made Child: Women-Centred Perspectives* (Clifton, N.J.: The Humana Press, Inc., 1981), p. 264.

[6] Joseph Fletcher, *The Ethics of Genetic Control: Ending Reproductive Roulette* (Garden City, N.J.: Anchor Books, 1974), p. 51.

[7] Ibid., p. 48.

[8] Bernard Nathanson, with Richard N. Ostling, *Aborting America* (Garden City, N.J.: Doubleday, 1979), p. 283.

[9] Shulamith Firestone, *The Dialectic of Sex: The Case for Feminist Revolution* (New York: Bantam Books, 1970), p. 241.

[10] Marge Piercy, *Woman on the Edge of Time* (New York: Ballantine Books, 1976), p. 102.

[11] Ibid., p. 105.

[12] Andrea Dworkin, *Right-Wing Women* (New York: G.P. Putnam and Son's, 1983), p. 188.

[13] Mary O'Brien, "Naming Our Experience," in *Healthsharing,* Summer 1983, p. 12.

[14] Mary O'Brien, "The Politics of Hysteria: Man, Media and the Test-Tube Baby," in *Canadian Women's Studies,* Summer 1979, p. 61.

[15] Ibid.

[16] O'Brien, "Naming Our Experience," p. 13.

CHAPTER EIGHT

[1] Connie Clement, "The Case for Lay Abortion," in *Healthsharing,* Winter 1983, p. 10.

[2] Linda Gordon, *Woman's Body, Woman's Right: A Social History of Birth Control in America* (New York: Grossman, 1976), p. 39.

[3] Ibid., p. 52.

[4] Lucinda Cisler, "Unfinished Business: Birth Control and Women's Liberation," in Robin Morgan, ed., *Sisterhood is Powerful* (New York: Random House, 1970), p. 260.

[5] Pauline Bart, "Seizing the Means of Reproduction: an illegal feminist abortion collective – how and why it worked," in Helen Roberts, ed., *Women, Health and Reproduction* (London: Routledge and Kegan Paul, 1981), pp. 121-122.

[6] Vicki Van Wagner, Letter in *Healthsharing*, Spring 1984, p. 26.

BIBLIOGRAPHY

Arditti, Rita, Renate Duelli Klein and Shelley Minden, eds. *Test-Tube Women*. London: Pandora Press, 1984.

Badgley, R.F., D.F. Caron and M.G. Powell. *Report of the Committee on the Operation of the Abortion Law*. Ottawa: Supply and Services Canada, 1977.

Bagne, Paul. "High-Tech Breeding," *Mother Jones*, August 1983.

Bart, Pauline. "Seizing The Means of Reproduction: an illegal feminist abortion collective – how and why it worked," in Helen Roberts, ed., *Women, Health and Reproduction*. London: Routledge and Kegan Paul, 1981.

Bernard, Jessie. *The Future of Motherhood*. New York: Penguin, 1974.

Borg, Susan and Judith Lasker. *When Pregnancy Fails*. Boston: Beacon Press, 1981.

Burtchaell, James T. *Rachel Weeping and Other Essays on Abortion*. Fairway, Kansas: Andrews and McNeel, 1982.

Callahan, Daniel. "Abortion: Some Ethical Issues," in Thomas A. Shannon, ed., *Bioethics,* rev. ed. Ramsey, N.J.: The Paulist Press, 1981.

Catano, Janis W. and Victor M. Catano. "Human Factors Applications to Childbirth Environments." Paper presented to Canadian Psychological Association, Montreal, 1982.

Chenier, Nancy Miller. *Reproductive Hazards at Work: Men, Women and the Fertility Gamble*. Ottawa: Canadian Advisory Council on the Status of Women, 1982.

Cisler, Lucinda. "Unfinished Business: Birth Control and Women's Liberation," in Robin Morgan, ed., *Sisterhood is Powerful*. New York: Random House, 1970.

Clement, Connie. "The Case for Lay Abortion," *Healthsharing*, Winter 1983.

Cole, Susan G. "The Real Abortion Issue," *This Magazine*, June 1983.

Collins, Larry D. "The Politics of Abortion: Trends in Canadian Fertility Policy," *Atlantis*, Spring 1982.

de Beauvoir, Simone. *The Second Sex*. New York: Alfred A. Knopf, 1952.

Devereux, George. *A Study of Abortion in Primitive Societies*. International Universities Press, 1955, 1976.

Doane, B.K. and B.G. Quigley. "Psychiatric Aspects of Therapeutic Abortion," *CMA Journal*, September 1, 1981.

Dworkin, Andrea. *Right-Wing Women*. New York: G.P. Putnam and Sons, 1983.

Ehrenreich, Barbara. *The Hearts of Men*. New York: Doubleday, 1983.

English, Deirdre. "The War Against Choice: Inside the Antiabortion Movement," *Mother Jones*, February/March 1981.

Fairweather, Eileen. "Abortion: The Feelings Behind the Slogans," *Spare Rib* 87.

Firestone, Shulamith. *The Dialectic of Sex: The Case for Feminist Revolution*. New York: Bantam Books, 1970.

Fletcher, Joseph. *The Ethics of Genetic Control: Ending Reproductive Roulette*. Garden City, N.J.: Anchor Books, 1974.

Francke, Linda Bird. *The Ambivalence of Abortion*. New York: Random House, 1978.

Francoeur, Robert T. *Utopian Motherhood: New Trends in Human Reproduction*. Garden City, N.J.: Anchor Books, 1974.

Gavigan, Shelley Ann Marie. *The Abortion Prohibition and the Liability of Women: Historical Development and Future Prospects*. Master of Laws Thesis. Toronto: Osgoode Hall Law School, York University, 1984.

Gilligan, Carol. *In a Different Voice: Psychological Theory and Women's Development*. Cambridge, Mass.: Harvard University Press, 1982.

Gordon, Linda. *Woman's Body, Woman's Right: A Social History of Birth Control in America*. New York: Grossman, 1976.

Greenglass, Esther R. *After Abortion*. Toronto: Longman Canada, 1976.

Greer, Germaine. *Sex and Destiny: The Politics of Human Fertility*. London: Secker and Warburg, 1984.

Hanmer, Jalna. "Sex predetermination, artificial insemination, and the maintenance of male-dominated culture," in Helen Roberts, ed., *Women, Health and Reproduction*. London: Routledge and Kegan Paul, 1981.

Harrison, Barbara Grizzuti. "On Reclaiming the Moral Perspective," *Ms*, June 1978.

The Human: A Magazine of Life Issues. Toronto: The Uncertified Human Publishing Co. Ltd.

Illich, Ivan. *Medical Nemesis: The Expropriation of Health.* London: Calder and Boyars, 1975.

Kitzinger, Sheila. *Women as Mothers.* Glasgow: Fontana Books, 1978.

Klaus, Marshall H. and John Kennell. *Maternal-Infant Bonding.* St. Louis, Mo.: C.V. Mosby Co., 1976.

Lader, Lawrence. *Abortion.* Boston: Beacon Press, 1966.

Matthews, Gwyneth Ferguson. *Voices from the Shadows: Women with Disabilities Speak Out.* Toronto: Women's Press, 1983.

McDonnell, Kathleen. "Claim No Easy Victories: The Fight for Reproductive Rights," in Maureen FitzGerald, Connie Guberman and Margie Wolfe, eds., *Still Ain't Satisfied: Canadian Feminism Today.* Toronto: Women's Press, 1982.

McLaren, Angus. "Birth Control and Abortion in Canada, 1870-1920," *Canadian Historical Review,* Vol. 59, No. 3 (1978).

Merton, Andrew H. *Enemies of Choice.* Boston: Beacon Press, 1981.

Morgentaler, Henry. *Abortion and Contraception.* Toronto: General Publishing, 1982.

Nathanson, Bernard and Richard N. Ostling. *Aborting America.* Garden City, N.J.: Doubleday, 1979.

O'Brien, Mary. "Naming Our Experience," *Healthsharing,* Summer 1983.

—— "The Politics of Hysteria: Man, Media and the Test-Tube Baby," *Canadian Women's Studies,* Summer 1979.

—— *The Politics of Reproduction.* London: Routledge and Kegan Paul, 1981.

Parvati, Jeanine. *Hygieia: A Woman's Herbal.* Berkeley, Calif.: Bookpeople, 1978.

Pelrine, Eleanor Wright. *Abortion in Canada.* Toronto: New Press, 1972.

Piercy, Marge. *Woman on the Edge of Time,* New York: Ballantine Books, 1976.

Rich, Adrienne. *Of Woman Born: Motherhood as Experience and Institution.* New York: Bantam Books, 1976.

"The Right to Grieve: Two Women Talk About Their Abortions," *Healthsharing,* Winter 1983.

Rorvik, David. *In His Image: The Cloning of a Man.* Philadelphia: J.P. Lippincott, 1978.

Ross, Val. "The pro-life boycott," *Maclean's,* January 30, 1984.

Rowbotham, Sheila. *Hidden from History.* London: Pluto Press, 1973.

Russ, Joanna. *The Female Man.* New York: Bantam, 1975.

Seaman, Barbara. *Women and the Crisis in Sex Hormones.* Brattleboro, Vt.: The Book Press, 1977.

Sumner, L.W. *Abortion and Moral Theory*. Princeton, N.J.: Princeton University Press, 1981.

The Vancouver Women's Health Collective. *Safe, Effective Birth Control Does Exist!* 1981. (Available from the V.W.H.C., 1501 West Broadway, Vancouver, B.C.)

Van Gelder, Lindsy. "Playboy's Charity: Is it Reparation or Rip-Off?" *Ms*, June 1983.

Verny, Thomas, M.D. with John Kelly. *The Secret Life of the Unborn Child*. Toronto: Collins, 1981.

Wade, Roger. *For Men, About Abortion*. 1978. (Available from Roger C. Wade, P.O. Box 4748, Boulder, Colo. 80306.)

Watters, Wendell W., M.D. *Compulsory Parenthood: The Truth About Abortion*. Toronto: McClelland and Stewart, 1976.

Watters, William and Peter Singer. *Test-Tube Babies*. Melbourne: Oxford University Press, 1982.

Zimmerman, Mary K. *Passage Through Abortion: The Personal and Social Reality of Women's Experience*. New York: Praeger, 1977.

—— "Psychosocial and Emotional Consequences of Elective Abortion: A Literature Review," in Paul Sachdev, ed., *Abortion: Readings and Research*. Toronto: Butterworths, 1981.

Zola, Irving Kenneth. "Medicine as an Institution of Social Control," in C. Cox and A. Mead, eds., *Sociology of Medical Practice*. New York: Collier MacMillan, 1975.

INDEX

Aborting America (Nathanson), 51,
    113
Abortion:
    aftereffects of, 33, 37, 59; see also
        Post-abortion grief
    ambivalence about, 28-31, 40,
        65, 66, 132
    availability of 17, 19, 33
    children's and adolescents'
        response to, 32-33
    class and, 70
    culture and, 70
    cutoff points for, 43-44
    economics and, 71
    fear of, 31, 65
    folk methods of, 127
    forced, 64
    medical control of, 125-26, 139
    for medical reasons, 35-36
    medical technology's effect on,
        24, 45
    opinion polls on, 20
    polarization on issue of, 17, 27-
        28, 48-49
    positive feelings about, 132
    regret over, 35
Abortion and Contraception (Morgen-
    taler), 46-47
Abortion Caravan, 19
Abortion clinics, 20, 134-36
Abortion counselling, 39, 65, 67,
    77
Abortion decisions:
    as learning process, 36-37, 38,
        40
    male role in, 63-66
    reasons for, 55
    "self versus other" dilemma in,
        30, 37-38
Abortion laws:

in Canada, 17-20, 44, 54, 56,
    63, 95, 126, 134
in England, 43-44
in Italy, 69
population control programs
    and, 96, 133
in United States, 17, 44, 126,
    134
Abortion, medical:
    safety of, 127
Abortion rights movement, 17-20,
    22, 28, 70, 88-89, 93-94,
    134-35;
    "choice" as strategy of, 68-70
    home birth movement and, 95,
        130-32
    lack of mass appeal of, 19, 24,
        28
    liberal humanist influence on,
        46-47
Adolescents' response to abortion,
    32-33
Adoption, 78-79
Alienation of men from reproduc-
    tion, 122-23
Ambivalence of Abortion, The
    (Francke), 30
Amniocentesis, 56, 75, 103, 104
Anderson, Doris, 82
Anniversary reactions to abortion,
    36
Anti-feminist women, 85-87
Anti-pregnancy vaccine, 100-101
Artificial insemination by donor
    (AID), 106
Artificial reproduction, 105-24

"Baby Doe," 89, 91
"Baby Jane Doe," 89

151

Badgley Committee on the Operation of the Abortion Law (1976), 19, 70
Barrier contraceptives, 98, 101
Bart, Pauline, 129
Bernard, Jessie, 72
Bioethics, 89, 107-8
Birth control: see Contraception
Birth control movement, medical opposition to, 126
Birth control pill, 98, 99
Bonding, maternal-infant, 32
Borowski, Joseph, 19, 20
Browne, Stella, 21

Callahan, Daniel, 54, 92-93, 103
Campaign Life, 82-83; see also Right-to-Life movement
Canadian Abortion Rights Action League (CARAL), 82; see also Abortion rights movement
"Case for Lay Abortion, The" (Clement), 125
Catano, Janis, 103, 127
Catholicism, 17, 43, 48, 85
Charney, Susan, 75-76
Chenier, Nancy Miller, 110
Childbearing, 62, 74, 121
Childbirth:
    medical control of, 101-3, 126, 139
    spiritual dimension of, 132
Childrearing:
    in industrial societies, 71-73
    lack of social support for, 72-74, 77
    sex roles in, 59, 62, 72-73
    in traditional societies, 72
Children's response to abortion, 32-33
Choice, ideology of:
    in abortion rights movement, 68-69, 131
    and feminist morality of abor-
tion, 55
    in home birth movement, 131
    in liberal democracies, 79
    and personal experience, 69
Choice, reproductive:
    cultural context of, 70, 74
    socioeconomic context of, 70-71, 74, 77
Christianity:
    moral philosophy on abortion, 42-43;
    see also Catholicism; Judaism; Protestantism
Cisler, Lucinda, 22, 129
Clement, Connie, 125, 131, 132
Cloning of a Man, The (Rorvik), 108
Cole, Susan G., 95-96, 97
Collins, Larry, 18
Compulsory Parenthood (Watters), 96
Conservatism, 17, 85-87; see also New Right
Contraception:
    doctors'; attitudes to, 97
    folk methods of, 127-28
    health hazards of, 98-99
    medical control of, 97, 98-101, 126, 139
    sexuality and, 98, 100
Counselling: see Abortion counselling; Genetic counselling; Pregnancy options counselling
Crean, Martha, 87-88
Criminal Code of Canada: see Abortion laws, in Canada

Dawson, Stephen, 90, 91
de Beauvoir, Simone, 21, 42-43, 60, 88
Depo Provera, 98, 99, 100, 110
Devereux, George, 42, 138
Devlin, Lloyd, 81
Desjardins, Larry, 84-85

Dialectic of Sex, The (Firestone), 114
Diethylstilbestrol *(DES)*, 110, 118
Disabled infants:
 lack of social support for, 76-77
Disabled rights movement:
 on medical treatment for dis-
  abled infants, 89
 Right-to-Life movement and,
  91
 on selective abortion, 56, 75-76
Doctors: *see* Medical establishment
Downer, Carol, 134
Dualistic view of human nature,
 120
Dworkin, Andrea, 54, 85, 87,
 118-19, 123

Ectogenesis, 108
Ehrenreich, Barbara, 59, 85, 86-
 87, 117
Electronic fetal monitoring (EFM),
 102
Enemies of Choice (Merton), 84, 87
English, Deirdre, 50, 80, 85-86,
 117
Ethic of care, 48, 49, 51, 57
Ethic of rights, 51, 53, 57
Eugenics, 74-75, 105, 111
Euthanasia, 90, 91

Fairweather, Eileen, 28
Family planning programs, 74,
 97, 101, 133
Fear of abortion, 31, 65
Fear of biological reproduction,
 113-14, 119-21
Female Man, The (Russ), 117
Feminist morality of abortion, 52,
 55-57, 61
Feminist Women's Health Center
 (Los Angeles), 134
Feminist Women's Health Center
 (Oakland, CA), 106

Fertility, values concerning, 27
Fetus:
 in feminist morality, 53-54
 identification with, 32-33, 87,
  92
 medical treatment of, 24, 104
 personhood of, 44, 46-47, 53-
  54
Finger, Anne, 89, 92
Finlayson, Judith, 83
Firestone, Shulamith, 114-15, 119
Fletcher, Joseph, 44, 105, 111-12,
 133
For Men, About Abortion (Wade), 65
Francke, Linda Bird, 30, 70
Francoeur, Robert, 112-13
Future of Motherhood, The (Bernard),
 72

Gale, Jane, 82, 83
Genetic abnormalities:
 cost-benefit analysis of, 75
 lack of social support for infants
  with, 77
Genetic engineering, 103-5
Genetic counselling, 104
Genetic screening, 104
Gilligan, Carol, 32, 37-38, 49-50,
 52
Goldman, Emma, 21
Gordon, Linda, 42, 127, 128
Graham, Robert, 105
Gray, Nellie, 87
Greenglass, Esther, 40
Greer, Germaine, 72, 74, 98, 101,
 138

Handler, Denyse, 87
Hardin, Garrett, 133
Health care system:
 social control function of, 97
Health professionals: *see* Medical
 establishment
Hearts of Men, The (Ehrenreich), 59

Hembree, Shirley, 50-51
Herbal abortifacients, 127, 128,
    138
Herbal contraceptives, 138; see also
    Contraception, folk methods
    of
Home abortion, 136-38
Home birth:
    legal status in Canada, 130, 131
    safety record of, 103, 127
Home birth movement, 103;
    and abortion rights movement,
    130-32
Homemaker's magazine, Campaign
    Life boycott of, 82-83
Hospital abortion committees, 13,
    18, 19, 95
Hospital birth:
    drugs used in, 102
    safety record of, 102, 103, 127
    stresses of, 135
Hospital boards, as Right-to-Life
    target, 19, 82
Hospital quota system for abor-
    tions, 18, 19
Human nature, dualistic view of,
    120
Humanism, 46-47
Hygieia: A Woman's Herbal (Par-
    vati), 138

Identification with the fetus, 32-
    33, 87, 92
Illegal abortion; 19-20
    safety record of, 128-30
    see also Abortion clinics; "Jane";
    Lay abortion
Illich, Ivan, 97
In a Different Voice (Gilligan), 32
In vitro fertilization, 106, 107-8,
    108-9
Infanticide, 42, 56, 90
Infertility, 78, 109-11, 117

Intrauterine device (IUD), 25, 44,
    98, 99, 110
Invasive contraceptives, 99-101

"Jane" (illegal abortion collective),
    129-30
Jefferson, Dr. Mildred, 87
Jiminez, Rosie, 69
Judaism, 48

Kennell, John, 32
Kitzinger, Sheila, 73
Klaus, Marshall, 32

Landolt, Gwen, 86
Landsberg, Michele, 47
Lay abortion, 126, 128;
    legal status of, 130, 131
    medical opposition to, 130
    safety record of, 127-30
    see also Illegal abortion; "Jane"
Legislation: see Abortion laws
Lejeune, Jerome, 54
Liberal democracies:
    ideology of choice in, 79
Liberal humanism, 46-47

Mandatory Motherhood (Hardin),
    133
Maternal-infant bonding, 32
Maternity leave, 73
Matthews, Gwyneth Ferguson, 76
McLaren, Angus, 128
Medhurst, Alexander, 63-64, 67
Medical establishment:
    biases, class and cultural, 74
    control of abortion by, 95-96,
    125-27
    control of reproduction by, 96-
    97, 108-9, 125-27, 132-
    33
Medical technology:
    effect on abortion issue, 24
    Right-to-Life support for, 92

see also Reproductive technology
Men:
  in abortion decisions, 61-67
  at abortion procedures, 66
  alienation from reproduction,
    122-23
  and childrearing, 58-60, 64, 73
  control of reproduction, 61, 63,
    111, 122-23
  feelings about abortion, 65-67
  reproductive responsibilities,
    58-59, 61-62
  "supportive man" role in abor-
    tion, 61, 64
  veto power over abortion, 25, 62
Menning, Barbara, 109, 111, 118
Menstrual extraction, 136
Mercy killing, 111
Merton, Andrew H., 84, 85, 87
Midwifery: *see* Home birth; Home
  birth movement
Moral philosophy:
  sex differences in, 49
  feminist approach to, 48, 52
Moral philosophy of abortion:
  medical technology and, 45
Moral philosophy, Western tradition of, 42-43;
  abstract orientation, 43, 44-45,
    52
  distrusted by feminists and pro-
    gressives, 46-47, 52
Morgentaler, Dr. Henry, 19-20,
  46-47, 51, 81, 84, 128
Morning-after pill, 25, 44, 110,
  118

Nathanson, Bernard, 44, 45, 51-
  52, 55, 113
New Right, 23, 93;
  Right-to-Life movement and,
    83-84, 85
  see also Conservatism

O'Brien, Mary, 119-21, 122, 123
Of Woman Born (Rich), 22
Opinion polls on abortion, 20

Parenting: *see* Childrearing
Parthenogenesis, 108, 116
Parvati, Jeanine, 138
Paternity, 122
Paternity leave, 73
Peace and non-violence:
  and abortion issue, 88
Pelrine, Eleanor Wright, 18
Pelvic Inflammatory Disease (PID),
  110
Personal experience, and beliefs
  about abortion, 51-52, 69
Personhood of the fetus, 44, 46-
  47, 53-54
Petrasek, Grace, 86
Piercy, Marge, 115-16, 119, 128
Pill, the, 98, 99
Playboy Foundation, 60
Politics of Reproduction, The
  (O'Brien), 120
Population control programs, 56,
  96-97, 133, 138
Post-abortion grief, 33-36, 54;
  in men, 66
  Right-to-Life movement and,
    23-24, 35, 40
  support needed for, 34, 36, 39
Post-partum depression, 33, 132
Pregnancy
  emotions during, 132
  physical changes during, 31
  wife-battering during, 63
Pregnancy options counselling, 77;
  see also Abortion counselling
Prenatal diagnosis, 75, 104
Pro-choice movement: *see* Abortion
  rights movement
Pro-life movement: *see* Right-to-
  Life movement

Productivity, as measure of human worth, 91
Progressive politics, and Right-to-Life movement, 84-85, 87-88
Prostaglandin suppositories, 136-37
Protestantism, 48
Psychic abortion, 138-39

Quality of life, 91-92
Quota system for hospital abortions, 18, 19

Rapp, Rayna, 76-77
Reagan, Ronald, 84
REAL (Realistic Equal Active for Life) Women, 86; see also Right-to-Life movement
Repeat abortions, 39
Repository for Germinal Choice, 105; see also Sperm banks
Reproduction:
    biological imbalance in, 62
    control of, 97, 112, 122, 123, 133, 139
    fear of, 113-14, 119-21
    male alienation from, 122-23
    utopian feminist visions of, 114-17, 136
    values concerning, 27, 121
Reproductive Hazards at Work (Chenier), 110
Reproductive rights, 25-26, 79-80, 133
Reproductive technology, 103-24;
    cafeteria approach to, 117
    control of, 117-18, 119-20
    effect on abortion issue, 24-26, 45-46
    feminist visions of, 114-24
    infertility and, 110-11
    as replacement for biological reproduction, 112-13

risks of, 117
    see also Medical technology
Rich, Adrienne, 22, 29, 103
Right-to-Life movement, 17, 22, 23, 27-28, 47-48, 55, 62, 78, 81;
    abortions obtained by members of, 50
    bioethics and, 89-90, 92, 107
    children's and adolescents' gravitation to, 32-33
    disabled rights movement and, 90, 91
    motivation for, 87-88, 93
    New Right and, 83-84
    progressive politics and, 84-85, 87-88
    Roman Catholic Church and, 48, 85
    tactics of, 19, 23, 35, 82-83
    women in, 85-88
Right-Wing Women (Dworkin), 54
Roman Catholic Church, 17, 43, 48, 85
Rorvik, David, 108
Russ, Joanna, 117

Sabia, Laura, 86
Sanger, Margaret, 126
Seaman, Barbara, 99
Second Sex, The (de Beauvoir), 21
Secret Life of the Unborn Child, The (Verny), 32
Selective abortion, 24, 56, 75-76, 96, 104; see also Eugenics
Self-abortion, 136-38
"Self versus other" dilemma in abortion decisions, 30, 37-38
Sex and Destiny (Greer), 72
Sex selection, 56, 104-5
Sexual conservatism, 84, 86-87
Sexual revolution, 60, 98
Sexual values, 27
Single mothers, 73-74

Sisterhood is Powerful, 22, 129
Social conservatism, 17, 85-87; *see also* New Right
Social control, as function of health care system, 97
Sperm banks, 105, 106
Sperm-splitting, 104-5
Sterilization:
    abuse of, 70
    in family planning programs, 101
Sumner, L.W., 44
Surrogate mothering, 106-7

Technology: *see* Medical technology; Reproductive technology
Test-tube babies: *see In vitro* fertilization
Therapeutic abortion committees, 13, 18, 19, 95
Trudeau, Pierre Elliott, 17
Turner, John, 18

Ultrasonography, 104
Utilitarian theory, 44
Utopian feminist visions of artificial reproduction, 114-17
Utopian Motherhood (Francoeur), 112

Value of human life, 90-91, 92
Van Gelder, Lindsy, 47
Van Wagner, Vicki, 72-73, 131-32
Vancouver Women's Health Collective (VWHC), 100, 101
Verny, Thomas, 32
Veto power over abortion, 62, 63
Voices from the Shadows (Matthews), 76

Wade, Roger, 65-66, 67
Wagner, Loretto, 87
Watters, Dr. Wendell, 96-97
Woman on the Edge of Time (Piercy), 115
Women and the Crisis in Sex Hormones (Seaman), 99
Women as Mothers (Kitzinger), 73
Women Exploited by Abortion, 35; *see also* Right-to-Life movement; Post-abortion grief
Women Unite, 21

Zola, Irving Kenneth, 97